Indoor Gardening
for Profit

Indoor Gardening
for Profit

ROY GENDERS

ROBERT HALE · LONDON

Robert Hale Ltd
Clerkenwell House
45–47 Clerkenwell Green
London EC1R 0HT

Photoset by Rowland Phototypesetting Ltd
Printed in Great Britain by
St Edmundsbury Press, Bury St Edmunds, Suffolk
and bound by Weatherby Woolnough

Contents

Illustrations

PICTURE CREDITS

The author thanks the following for permission to reproduce illustrations: ICI Ltd (1 and 5); Bainbridge Engineering Ltd (2); Monsanto Chemicals Ltd (4); Pat Brindley (6 and 59); John Gledhill (10, 12, 18, 19, 21, 25, 26, 30, 36–40, 43, 44, 46, 47, 49, 50, 52, 54–7); and Sutton & Sons Ltd (42)   The line drawings are by Steven Charlton.

1

An Introduction to Gardening Indoors

Earning money at home—Where to grow plants—Methods of heating—Selling your produce—Equipment

There must be many people today with spare time at home, such as married women with young children to look after who cannot go out to work in the daytime or those looking after an invalid parent, who would enjoy taking up a profitable hobby to augment the family income or simply to occupy their time. There are also those who through infirmity or illness are unable to follow an occupation away from home but who would be able to do so in their own home, even if confined to a wheelchair, if they have the use of their hands. There are single people too, who could do their indoor gardening at weekends or in the evenings to earn extra money, and there is nothing more rewarding than growing things—raising plants from seed or from cuttings and this is especially so if one is able to profit from a spare-time occupation. There are many instances of a hobby becoming a highly profitable business in a very short time. There was the case of the lady who has built up a large business with world-wide sales, growing and propagating herbs in her Cambridgeshire garden which is now so famous that it is open to the public during the summer months; and the Essex lady who has, in a few years, built up an international reputation for growing unusual garden plants. But this is a book on gardening indoors, in the home, or by using a small greenhouse or garden room, cellar or shed. Within the past decade, one has read of the young married woman who began growing the popular African violet in her cellar, entirely under artificial lighting and soon became so successful that her ability to grow these plants to perfection brought her a world-wide reputation so that in addition to the profitable sales from her plants, she wrote several books and contributed to many publications throughout the English-speaking world on her favourite flower as well as being in great demand as a lecturer.

Then there were the three middle-aged ladies who set up in business as mushroom growers. One had been left a widow with quite a young family to bring up; another was divorced; the third one had time on her hands, being the wife of a successful businessman who spent much of the year abroad for his firm. The three of them began in an old barn situated at the bottom of the garden of the home of one of them and, after obtaining professional advice, set up as mushroom growers, obtaining help in the preparation of the compost, spawning the beds and marketing the crop for their first year. At the end of this time, they were thoroughly efficient in the business and went from strength to strength, later taking over an old mill and earning a very large income.

There are many ways of earning money from gardening at home but it is necessary to select for one's hobby a plant that you like and then to grow and market it better than anyone else. The best plants to grow are "collector's" plants, those which by their diversity or form or colour, endear themselves to growers who are always on the look-out for a new variety to add to their collection. There are also plants of especially easy culture. One could mention cacti and other succulents such as sempervivums, handsome in their foliage; also miniature roses; Rex begonias with their amazing metallic colourings and leaf variations; the interesting scented-leaf geraniums; and African violets. Each of these plants is of easy culture and for some years now has enjoyed considerable popularity. They are plants that are best grown indoors (though miniature roses are sufficiently hardy for planting in the open) where the leaf variations attract much attention and usually sell on sight when displayed in florists' windows. Nor are they overdone like some indoor plants such as the dwarf pot chrysanthemums which, by controlling the light, are grown in their millions by specialists and marketed all the year round. These are not plants for the home grower.

The plants to grow are those that the large commercial growers find too labour intensive or that need that little extra care in their propagation and culture which the large commercial grower cannot devote to them. It is also important to grow plants that do not require large amounts of artificial heat in their rearing for all forms of heating are now expensive and unless plants requiring considerable heat can be grown on an extensive scale, there will be no profit in their production. Only those plants requiring the minimum of heat should be grown.

Where to grow plants

It is important to decide which is the most suitable plant to grow when taking into consideration available facilities. There may be a cellar beneath one's home which may no longer be filled with tons of coal to burn on the kitchen range and now lies empty but which could be brought into profitable use for growing mushrooms or African violets under artificial light. There may be an outhouse with an old copper boiler where once the washing was done and which may be suitable for growing sempervivums in small pots or they could be grown in garden frames in an asphalted courtyard where there is no garden at all. The plants are hardy and readily propagated by offsets. What is more, the frames can be left open all summer and if one has to be away from home for any length of time, the plants will take no harm as they need little moisture. Being succulents, they are able to store up large amounts of water in their foliage. Or ask a friend or neighbour to water them once each week if the weather is dry. One's movements will decide which plants to grow for some require almost hourly attention, whilst others can be put out in frames after potting them indoors and left to take care of themselves. Miniature roses and sempervivums in small pots can occupy the frames all the year if necessary, requiring no winter heat. Pots of bulbs such as snowdrops and *Iris reticulata*, both possessing extreme hardiness, will also be kept outdoors until they bloom and are sold in February or March straight from the frames, whilst hyacinths and Christmas tulips require some warmth to bring them into bloom for it is at Christmas that they are most wanted. Rex begonias and scented-leaf geraniums require nothing more than to be grown on in a room where the winter temperature does not fall below 50°F (10°C), though they should be protected from winter damp by providing them with a dry atmosphere.

It is advisable to concentrate on just one plant and to grow it and market it better than anyone else. Begin by obtaining as many varieties as possible as stock plants and perhaps have a small catalogue printed, though most of one's plants will now be sold through local retailers situated in a town rather than by post. Before making a start, it will be advisable to visit your florist. Take a plant with you to show what one intends to grow and find the most suitable selling times for a particular plant, though for cacti in small pots or made up into miniature gardens there is an all-year demand. Several of our largest growers of cacti began with a few plants in the kitchen or in a sunny attic, then progressed to a small greenhouse or sun room, then to a larger-size greenhouse at a later date, eventually building up a national reputation as a grower of these plants. African violets, Rex begonias and scented-leaf geraniums also have year-round sales.

There is a considerable demand today for well-grown pot plants of all descriptions from those exhibiting at Chelsea and other large flower shows and at the Ideal Home Exhibition; and from banks and hotels for displaying to their customers. Plants in pots are preferred to cut flowers for they last longer and are more economic, whilst they also need less attention. Well-grown plants of Rex begonia and scented-leaf geraniums always find a ready sale with hotels and restaurants, also with banks and offices which are empty during weekends, for these plants require watering perhaps only once each week. Many of the exotic-looking plants purchased for indoor decoration require a home with efficient central heating to be long-living and are produced by specialist growers on a large scale who have heated glasshouses kept at the correct heat and humidity to meet the plants' requirements. But there are other plants within the cultural range of the amateur grower who has only a small greenhouse or maybe only a frame at his or her disposal, or perhaps an attic or basement. The plants can be propagated sitting at a bench in the kitchen or scullery, in an outhouse or garden shed. They can then be moved outside to a frame. An invalid can do the propagating, by means of cuttings or offsets and the plants removed outdoors by a member of one's family or a friend. Even when one is perhaps not well enough to travel to work, it may be possible to tend the plants in the garden or courtyard, removing the frame lights on warm days and replacing them at night, to protect the plants from the cold, whilst a few minutes could be given once or twice a day to attend to the plants' watering and spraying. When the plants are ready for sale, perhaps the local florist will collect them and pay for them at the same time. It is important to maintain regular supplies for a florist may build up a steady demand for one's produce and will search elsewhere for supplies of a good selling line if your own is not available.

High postal costs now prevent the mail-order sale of plants from pots which have a large amount of soil at their roots but one may be able to sell cuttings of certain plants for people to propagate and grow on their own. Cuttings of miniature roses and of scented-leaf geraniums, or the leaves of African violets can be sent by first-class letter post at reasonable charges. The cuttings should be packed in damp moss and placed in a small plastic bag to prevent moisture evaporation should they be delayed in the post. Goods sent by post should be despatched during the first three days of the week to ensure their delivery before the weekend, otherwise they may be left several days in a poorly ventilated sorting office.

To make a start with indoor gardening for profit, remember that one should grow only those plants that will flourish under the conditions available. The Rex begonias and scented-leaf geraniums do not require maximum amounts of sunlight as do pinks and carnations, violets and sun roses which are plants for outdoors. Miniature roses require sunlight but will flower well in a sunny window and can be grown on in a frame after their propagation indoors. Cacti and bonsai gardens can be made up indoors, and grown on in a sun room which is now an adjunct to many homes. There may also be room to erect a lean-to greenhouse against a sunny courtyard wall which will enable all manner of plants to be propagated. The lean-to made of bronzed aluminium and manufactured by Florada Garden Products of Cirencester is both elegant and efficient as a plant house or a sun-room extension to one's home. Edenlite Products of Hawksworth, Wiltshire, also make a splendid lean-to in rust-proof aluminium which is of modular construction and can be extended to any length. They also manufacture the orthodox greenhouse which has a steel base for durability. Most modern greenhouses are fitted with sliding doors with finger-tip control and do not catch the wind when opened. They can be left ajar if it is required to admit fresh air. Crittal-Hope make an efficient lean-to, complete with staging supports and shelf brackets. The metal is protected from corrosion by the hot-dip galvanizing process.

An inexpensive structure is that made by Garden Relax Ltd of Rainham, Essex, and which consists of a strong galvanized metal frame which is fixed into the ground and over it is placed Hi-

This small greenhouse, manufactured by Lawrence Gray Ltd using ICI Novolux PVC sheeting, can be erected in thirty minutes

clarity ICI plastic sheeting. It is shatter-proof and should be used where there is low-flying aircraft. There is built-in ventilation and staging is provided. The greenhouse takes only a few minutes to erect.

A simple lean-to structure may be erected using 2-inch timber for the uprights and roof and covering the structure with PVC sheeting or with Screenet, a polythene sheeting reinforced with wire netting. A simple door is made from builders' laths and which is fixed to one upright by means of strong hinges. Such a structure can be made for about £20 and will give several years' use.

Methods of heating

To heat a small greenhouse, if adjoining the house, you can use electricity. An efficient heater is the Autoheat, manufactured by Findlay, Irvine Ltd of Penicuik, Lothian. The 3000-watt model will heat a greenhouse 12 feet by 8 feet and a built-in thermometer and thermostat ensures efficient running and low costs. The heater is made of rigid PVC and will not rust, whilst all metal parts are earthed.

Ekco market efficient heaters for placing beneath a greenhouse bench. They are rust- and drip-proof and carry a load of 60 watts per foot. They are obtainable up to 12 feet in length.

Modern paraffin heaters are an efficient alternative and those manufactured by Aladdin are most reliable. The No. 2 Blue-flame burner model will heat a greenhouse of 100 cubic feet at a cost of about 5p per hour. Their Maxi-heater unit with its 5-gallon paraffin tank will provide heat for a week without refilling. Keep the wick trimmed regularly, then they will not smoke.

Where there is room outdoors, a simple frame can be constructed by cementing together three rows of bricks to the dimensions of 5 feet by 3 feet frame light. This will be made of wood and glass or of heavy-grade PVC. The "All Seasons" garden frames made by Bainbridge Engineering Ltd of Bury,

The Bainbridge "All Seasons" garden frame with sliding panels of ICI Novolux, a long-lasting PVC material. This frame can be erected on terrace or verandah if no garden is available

Lancashire, is to be recommended to those who raise plants in pots. They can be erected almost anywhere and measure 57 inches by 36 inches and 29 inches by 36 inches and are 15 inches deep at the back. They are made of high-purity aluminium and are flanged for additional strength. They are also insulated on the inside with expanded polystyrene. Easily erected, the sides bolt together with aluminium nuts and bolts and the frames are secured to the ground with anchor pegs. The sliding-top panels provide easy access and controlled ventilation and are made of long-lasting clear corrugated Novolux, a PVC material manufactured by ICI. The frames can be moved around, without dismantling, by two people. The frame may be placed on a terrace or verandah within easy reach of the house; or in a sunny basement courtyard.

The great value of this type of cold frame is that the expanded polystyrene insulation ensures that the frame retains the maximum amount of warmth during sunny days and heat-loss during the night is kept to a minimum.

If constructing a frame over a soil base, four lengths of boarding can be used, cut to the size of the light and held in place by strong stakes driven into the ground. Transparent polythene sheeting is used for the light, fixed to builders' laths. Claritex has earned a high reputation for light transmission and durability.

Where an electric supply is available, the use of warming wires and cables placed 12 inches beneath the surface of the soil will turn the cold frame into a heated "greenhouse" and enable cuttings to be rooted and wide range of plants to be raised. A transformer unit which reduces the mains supply to a safe low voltage is used to heat a plastic-covered galvanized wire buried beneath a bed of soil or sand.

To make a sand-propagating frame in a cold greenhouse (which will reduce the heating bills considerably), construct a wooden box of 9-inch boards and line the base with thick felt. Over it, place a 2-inch layer of washed sand and then the warming wires (allowing 8 watts per square foot of sand). Over the wires, place another 3 inches of sand and on this will stand the seed boxes or pots. A soil thermostat is necessary to control the temperature of the unit.

The use of soil-warming cables in a greenhouse, for propagation or growing on plants such as cacti and indoor bulbs, will enable the air temperature to be kept at a minimum and be more economic. The bottom heat generated by the cables will maintain plant growth when outside winter temperatures are low. A low-voltage transformer which reduces the mains supply to a safe voltage is used to heat plastic-covered galvanized wire placed beneath a bed or soil or sand. Bottom heat is more efficient than top heat in plant propagation.

A propagating unit can also be used to raise all manner of seedlings including tomatoes, aubergines, cucumbers and melons, some of which may be grown on in the greenhouse during summer when it is not needed for propagating. The Humex automatic propagator measuring 36 inches by 20 inches by 12 inches deep is highly efficient for on a 40-watt consumption running costs are less than 25p a week. The unit is constructed of fibreglass whilst the temperature is regulated by a rod-type thermostat which is adjusted to provide any temperature up to 180°F (82°C). For safety, the low-voltage heating wire is enclosed in a layer of sand.

Whilst much of the work can be done in the home, in a kitchen, lighted cellar or attic, a small greenhouse or frame may be necessary to grow on certain plants or bulbs. Frames can be kept in use throughout the year. Bulbs can be brought early into bloom in a frame even without artificial heat when they will make top prices in the shops. Another frame can be filled with alpine plants in small pots to be made up into miniature gardens indoors, using plastic or earthenware bowls. These, when made up, are placed in the frame cleared of bulbs when in bloom and which would have occupied the frame for several weeks. Small alpine gardens always sell readily, to give as presents or to decorate a dining table. No artificial heat is required in the culture of alpine plants. Cacti can also be grown in a warm frame and used to make into miniature gardens, whilst the closely related sempervivums require no heat at all.

Variegated-leaf Rex begonias and scented-leaf geraniums, both happier in diffused light than in full sunlight, can be propagated and grown in an attic which has one or more sky-lights. If the roof has been insulated (and it should have been to conserve the warmth of the house) it may not be necessary to use artificial heat for warm air rises and the attic of a centrally heated house is usually warm even if it has no form of heating itself. If more warmth is needed, this may be provided by a small tubular heater working off the mains.

Selling Your Produce

The atmosphere of an attic is dry and is not suitable for propagating African violets which require a moister atmosphere, a cellar being ideal. Here they can be grown under fluorescent lighting, standing the pots on trays of pebbles kept constantly moist. So before making a choice of which plant it is hoped to specialize in, available conditions must be considered. It is advisable to visit one or two growers who are usually only too willing to help a newcomer who may eventually be a customer for plants or cuttings. There are firms specializing in the sale of Rex begonia and African violet leaves for propagating and in the sale of young cacti for growing on in pots. The names of the specialist growers can be obtained through the gardening Press or by writing to the editor of the garden magazines who will usually be able to help in putting the enthusiast in touch with established growers. A small stock of plants (or their leaves or cuttings for rooting) will need to be purchased and the outlay will depend upon the plants to be grown. If it is intended to produce miniature roses in small pots—and these delightful plants are enjoying considerable popularity—ten or twelve different varieties can be obtained to grow on as stock plants from which to take cuttings. Perhaps four plants of each will give a worthwhile number of cuttings in their second year and the stock plants can be grown outdoors in large pots.

Cacti and sempervivums can be purchased in small pots or raised from seed. They are grown on and sold in pots or used to make miniature gardens which are sold through local florists, though a small advertisement in the local weekly paper which usually has a long life and wide readership will often bring many orders for indoor gardens to give as presents. Those with transport will collect when ready and so will the florist if not too distant. The correct presentation of the plants will be described in each chapter for it is important that, having raised plants of top quality, they should not be spoilt by poor presentation. Raising the plants is only half-way to success, their presentation in a professional manner is equally important. Your ability to do so will bring in many more enquiries for plants by word of mouth of satisfied customers and upon this, a profitable business is built up.

Besides making early contact with your local florists, there may be a supermarket close at hand who might take well-grown pot plants to sell and a visit will be worthwhile, taking a sample of the plants you have grown and showing how they will be presented. Also call at any nearby banks and building societies, hotels and restaurants who all use pot plants to brighten their surroundings and to attract customers. The inclusion of an advertisement at certain times of the year in your local newspaper will bring the plants to the attention of buyers who are always on the look-out for well-grown pot plants and miniature gardens to give as presents at Christmas and for birthdays. Pots of hyacinths and tulips should be ready to meet the Christmas demand and miniature gardens too sell well at this time. Evening callers for your plants will not take up too much time and this is a time of day which is convenient for people. Let them see your plants growing and their quality. Make their visit as interesting as possible and they will pass this on to their friends. In this way, a profitable private demand for plants will be built up.

I well remember starting mushroom growing in the cellar of my home in the early 1930s, when indoor mushroom culture was in its infancy in Britain and the use of pure culture spawn was just beginning. Many people would call for a quarter of mushrooms (6d then), simply to see them growing. The beds were covered in snow-white clumps, some 12 inches across, and created much interest. The visitors knew that the mushrooms were as fresh as could be for they could see them being picked straight from the bed and soon a valuable customer trade was built up.

Equipment

The minimum of equipment will be needed for growing plants at home rather than in the garden. A supply of pots is the main consideration and these are obtainable from wholesalers. Nowadays, most plant containers are plastic rather than earthenware and are less expensive to buy and lighter to move about. They can also be more easily stored in an attic, cellar or garden shed.

One will need a strong bench or table for propagation and potting the plants and a watering-can is essential but except for a dibber for transplanting, a knife for taking cuttings, and a trowel for potting plants, little else is necessary, apart from suitable composts. The materials needed for growing a particular plant

Two types of growing trays. *Above*: Vacapaks are plastic trays divided into sections. They are placed in a seed box for rigidity and the seedlings are transplanted directly into them and grown on. There is no disturbance when the plants are moved to pots. *Below*: A rigid seed tray which can be separated into individual packs by removing the tape

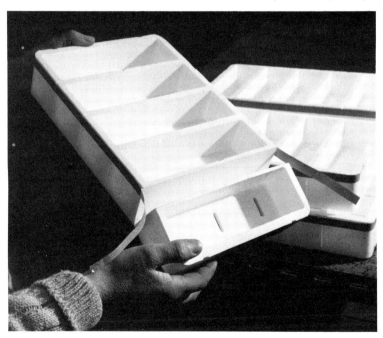

are given in each chapter and they may be kept in a cellar or shed, or beneath the bench of a small greenhouse if the work is to be done there. The ingredients for potting composts are clean to use and are without any unpleasant smell. They are obtainable from sundries shops or garden centres, usually in 56-pound bags and most trades people will deliver for a small extra charge.

Sterilized soil is obtainable from most nurserymen but it is as well to order your requirements in plenty of time so that the nurserymen can sterilize an extra amount of soil when preparing his own. Most plants are rooted in sand and peat, both of which are free of pest and disease spores present in unsterilized soil and these materials are used for propagating purposes. If sterilized soil is not easily obtainable, use soil from pasture land which has not grown arable crops for some time. Again, it is possible to have this delivered for a small extra cost. Good soil is often advertised in the local Press.

Automatic watering trays, by which plants in pots or boxes are placed on layers of felt or other moisture holding materials which are kept constantly moist, are a boon to those who have to be away from home for lengthy periods. Moisture is regulated from the tank

Do not attempt to grow too many things at the beginning. It is better to concentrate on one line and to do it well. In this way, you will build up a reputation for a particular plant. Then, when one has become efficient in the culture of a certain plant, and there will be difficulties and disappointments when beginning (for growing plants is similar to cooking), another line can be added. If possible, take up a plant that can be produced and sold all the year round, such as African violets or mushrooms in a cellar or outhouse, or Rex begonias in the home, so that there will be no long periods without something to sell. These days a regular income is all-important.

It may be that with the ever-increasing cost of travel to and from work, more and more people will choose to work at home. Soon we may see the spinning-wheel in action again in some remote cottage or a more sophisticated method of spinning and weaving that can be practised at home, and besides the culture of plants, the housewife, with less work available to her in the factory or office, will turn again to the life of earlier times, when bread was baked at home and sold to one's neighbours and jams and pickles for sale were prepared on the kitchen cooker.

This is a book for those who have little or no garden, possibly only a tiny basement or courtyard where a small greenhouse can be erected, or a terrace or verandah on which is placed a garden frame. But most of the work can be done indoors, in the comfort of one's home where full use can be made of its heating and lighting in the growing of plants, and from their sales, the money can be used to pay the bills.

2

The African Violet

Its discovery—Cultural requirements—Leaf propagation—
Rooting composts—Growing on the plants—Propagation
by division—Growing from seed—Pests and Diseases—
Varieties

Many houses built during Victorian times and before 1940, when
coal was inexpensive and widely used for open fires, had a cellar
or basement for storing coal and wood. Today the cellar mostly
stands empty of everything but unwanted boxes and jam jars
when it could be put to better use. It is not generally realized that
there is one beautiful flowering plant, the African violet, that can
be grown entirely under artificial light. It need never see sunlight
or even the light of day and indeed actually grows better when it
does not.

The plant was discovered in 1892 by the German botanist
Baron von Saint Paul-Illaire during a plant-finding expedition to
East Africa where he came upon it in the rain forests near the
Equator. It grows naturally nowhere else. This will give a clue as
to its cultural requirements—a humid atmosphere and shielded
from the direct rays of the sun. It was named African violet by its
finder for it is low growing like the European violet and the single
flowers of the species are deep violet-blue. As it was found on the
African continent, what better name than African violet whilst its
botanical name, *Saintpaulia*, was given to it in honour of its finder.
The Baron sent seeds to several European nurserymen and the
following year it was exhibited at the Ghent Floral Exhibition in
Belgium. By the end of the century, plants were being shown at
horticultural exhibitions throughout Europe but it was the
American firm of Armacost & Royston of Los Angeles, a town
closely associated with the Hollywood film industry and at the
time growing in size more rapidly than any other city in the

United States, which first took up its culture commercially and made the African violet well known. For centuries it had remained undetected in its native land but at once the Los Angeles nursery firm realized they had a winner for it lends itself to hybridizing more than any other indoor plant and soon they had raised plants with flowers of many glorious new colours. Some were pink, others blue with an edging of white. One had flowers of royal blue; another of sky blue and there were others in shades of crimson, carmine and wine red. The blooms too, increased in size from those of the original which were the size of an old 6d piece. Some were double, whilst others had attractively waved petals. What is more, it was found that the plants bloomed continuously under correct conditions, at the same time retaining their compact habit. The flowers are borne in short trusses of up to ten or more blooms and appear amongst the leaves or just above them. Happy in small pots, the plants can be flowered on glass shelves in any room lit by artificial lighting which exactly controls their growth and flowering. They were just the plants for a high-rise flat or city apartment for they took up little space and demanded the minimum of care in their culture. They were soon to occupy a permanent place in the rooms of many a Hollywood film star and the popularity of the little charmers spread across America. By the end of the 1920s, Armacost & Royston were producing and selling tens of thousands each year for the plants soon became collector's items and whenever they introduced a new variety, it was assured of big sales. By the end of the next decade, the firm had more than an acre under glasshouse cultivation and they were sending plants to all parts of the world. But it was not until the post-war years (the late 1940s) that the little plant took on a similar popularity in Europe. Until then most house plants were grown only in conservatories attached to large country houses. They were thought to be difficult to manage until their culture was taken up by several large firms who educated the public to their easy management. By the early 1950s, several firms began specializing in African violets for with the conversion of many older houses into flats, this was an ideal plant for decoration, taking up little space and flowering the whole year round. What is more, the greater use of central heating now provided more suitable conditions for growing plants indoors. The entire house had a greater warmth and was free of draughts and the correct humidity could be provided for the violets by standing the pots on trays of small stones kept constantly moist. By the end of the 1950s, the plant had become as popular in Britain and across northern Europe as it was in the USA and African violet or Saintpaulia societies were inaugurated, stimulating interest in the plant still further. The demand for the plant in its many lovely forms continues unabated and anyone with a cellar beneath their home could turn it to profitable account by their culture. The work is in no way difficult or arduous and it is most rewarding not only financially but in satisfying the natural desire of everyone to produce something of beauty. The daintiness and clarity of colour of the flowers have more than anything brought about its popularity. To the town dweller it has replaced the violet of the hedgerow, now rapidly vanishing from the countryside. So great is its popularity in the USA that there are now more than 2,000 varieties, though only a small proportion of these are grown in Britain.

The plant is of the same family, Gesneraceae, as the gloxinia and achimene, both of which are grown from corms and need considerable heat to grow well. At one time they were to be found in every Edwardian conservatory but with the high cost of heating today they have lost much of their popularity. And whilst the achimene and gloxinia die back after flowering and require a rest before they are brought into growth again, the Saintpaulia is both evergreen and continuous in flower. The plant has spoon-shaped leaves about 2 inches (5 centimetres) across which grow from a central crown and they are deeply grooved, to enable moisture to drain quickly from them in the rain forests of their native land. The dark green of the leaves of most varieties enhances the clarity of the flowers and even when not in bloom for short periods, the plants have a certain charm.

Cultural Requirements

They do not enjoy strong sunlight but may be grown on the window sill of an east- or west-facing room where they receive early-morning or late-evening sunlight but a south-facing window must be avoided. A simple test is to hold the hand about 4 inches (10 centimetres) above the plant and if the light casts a slight shadow, this is the correct amount of light they must have but not direct sunlight for long periods. There is no denying that African violets grow best under artificial lighting, though too strong lighting will scorch the leaves just as the direct rays of the midday sun will. The plants may be grown in any living-room, perhaps in an alcove fitted with glass shelves, lighted by concealed fluorescent lighting which makes a pleasing alternative to a display of glass or china. As they are grown in small pots, about six plants may be placed on a 2-foot (60-centimetre) shelf of plate glass and these can be arranged one above another spaced 12 inches (30 centimetres) apart. However dark the room, it can be made suitable for African violets and this is where the cellar or basement comes in. A basement will have a small window and often has ready access to the street so that composts, pots and other equipment can be taken down without going into the house. Many cellars also have one or more windows above ground level which give ready access and provide ample ventilation. There are cellars entirely without windows and these can be used to propagate African violets equally well. A cellar is an ideal place for propagating the plants for the necessary degree of humidity can be readily maintained throughout the year and fluorescent lighting provided.

To obtain the maximum number of plants in the cellar, benches can be erected around the walls, 3 to 4 feet (1 metre) above the floor and from the ceiling, some 2 feet (60 centimetres) above the benches, additional plants can be grown on trays placed on lengths of timber which are suspended from the ceiling by strong chains. Each 6-foot (2-metre)-long tray with plants growing on the bench is lighted by an 80-watt fluorescent tube fitted to a 6-foot (2-metre) reflector. This is suspended 12 inches (30 centimetres) above the plants, 100 of which in their small pots can be accommodated in each tray so that many hundreds can be grown in quite a small cellar. The pots are stood on metal trays covered with small pebbles. These are kept constantly moist so as to provide the necessary humidity. The lights are switched on at 8 a.m. and turned off at 10 p.m. which gives 14 hours of lighting and is the minimum necessary for healthy plant growth. Provide them with an extra hour or two daily if possible.

No great amount of heat is required. The lights will give off enough to raise the air temperature by several degrees and being below ground or partly so, a cellar will be warmer than other unheated rooms in the house in winter and will be cooler in summer.

A 4-foot-long electrically operated thermotube fitted with a thermostat as manufactured by Ekco will be sufficient to raise the winter temperature of a cellar 18 feet by 12 feet by 8 feet high to 58°–60°F (15°–16°C) which is ideal for African violets. If the room is larger, use two heating tubes, or one of greater length. The tubes are made of durable aluminium and have die-cast terminal chambers. They can be mounted singly or in twos and generate 60 watts per foot of tube. For temperature stability and economy, it is advisable to fit a thermostat. Like the tubes, it will be drip-proof and will switch off the heating tubes when the cellar is at the required maximum temperature of 60°F (16°C) and switch on when the temperature falls to 56°F (14°C). The plants will respond to an almost constant temperature which is the same whether growing in a cellar or when flowering in the living-room. African violets do not require excessive temperature, but a constant one and with some degree of humidity. The flower buds will fall if the air temperature is too dry. The plants will tolerate a day temperature of up to 70°F (20°C) but no higher than 56°F (14°C) at night.

Humidity is provided by standing the plants in their pots on trays of moist pebbles, or on a saucer of pebbles kept continually moist. The plants enjoy a steamy atmosphere and bloom well in a kitchen or bathroom where they may also be kept on glass shelves. If using pebbles, keep them nicely moist but the temperature must be such that there is always moisture evaporation. The plants should not stand in stagnant water for any length of time or they will damp off.

Leaf Propagation

To obtain a stock, a number of the specialist growers sell leaves from which young plants are propagated; or well-grown stock plants can be purchased from a wholesale grower or garden centre and from them a number of leaves are removed every month. This is the way to perpetuate the named varieties but plants may also be raised from seed.

Leaves are sent by 1st class post for they are light in weight and to prevent moisture evaporation, they are packed in polythene bags. Commercial growers will obtain the leaves in batches of 10 to 100 of a named variety though African violet collectors may wish to order in only twos and threes. There are growers who cater for their requirements and charge accordingly for the additional packing. Where leaf propagating facilities are not available, specialists send out plantlets which are rooted leaf cuttings. Young plants from small pots are best sent by British Rail. They are packed in open-top boxes covered with plastic sheeting to protect the plants from the draughts and cold wind.

The leaves, which are almost round and of the size of a dessert spoon, are removed from the plants with care, so as not to upset the balance. June and July is the best time for rooting, though they will root any time provided a temperature of 60°F (16°C) can be maintained for 4–5 weeks. The leaves should be fresh and free of blemishes. They should be neither too large nor too small, and should have the full length of the petiole or leaf stalk attached. This is inserted into the rooting medium in a wide-topped plastic pot (as used for bulbs) or in a seed tray, making them firm in the compost and setting them about 2 inches (5 centimetres) apart. The leaf stalk is planted 1 inch (2.5 centimetres) deep with the blade in an upright position. If the blades flop over, insert a few small sticks to keep them upright. Rooting will be more rapid if the base of each petiole is split to about ½ inch up before planting but if this is done, greater care is needed in their planting. If the

Propagating African violets from leaf cuttings

leaves show signs of "flagging", stand them in a cup of water for an hour before planting, with the base of the petioles just covered with water. Selection of the leaves is all-important, for older leaves take longer to root whilst small, young leaves produce plants of inferior quality.

Where there is no cellar or suitable place for large-scale propagation, leaves can be rooted in small jam jars filled with water and placed in the window of a warm room where diffused sunlight can enter. But never stand them in full sun. If you do, the leaves will become scorched.

For the leaves to stand upright, tie a piece of plastic over the top of the jar and make several holes just large enough for the leaf stalks to be inserted through them into the water. Use a separate jar for each variety. Almost the entire length of the petiole should be immersed in water and take care to see that the water level is maintained for the leaves are heavy drinkers. If it is possible to obtain rain water, this is preferable to using tap water which may be of high chlorination. It has also been observed that leaves will root faster in coloured glass jars than in clear glass but coloured jars are now more difficult to obtain. In water, leaves will normally root in about 3–4 weeks and will usually take an extra 2 weeks to root in sand or John Innes compost.

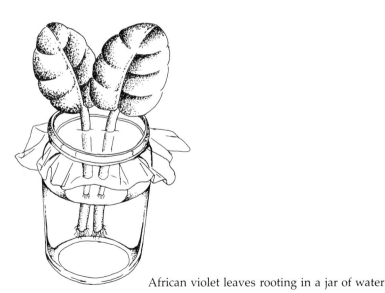

African violet leaves rooting in a jar of water

Rooting Composts

A mixture of sand and moist peat in equal parts by bulk will prove a suitable rooting medium and has the advantage in that it is soil-less, for unless the soil has been sterilized it may contain disease spores which will cause the leaves to damp off. A mixture of vermiculite and moist peat is equally suitable and this too will contain no disease spores. For this reason, peat should be used instead of leaf mould. For rooting, an "open" compost or rooting medium is essential. This will allow surplus moisture to drain quickly away and allows the roots freedom to spread out. Another alternative is to use the John Innes compost as recommended for sowing seeds. It is obtainable at garden centres everywhere and is prepared to a recognized formula. The soil will have been sterilized. But sand and moist peat is equally reliable and African violets enjoy a neutral or slightly acid soil and grow well where there is some peat in their diet. There should be a 2-inch (5-centimetre) depth of compost to take almost the full length of petiole (leaf stalk) which will give the leaves rigidity. If a plastic seed tray is used, set them about 1 inch (2.5 centimetres) apart in rows.

Keep the compost comfortably moist but not wet and to prevent it drying out too quickly and too rapid evaporation of moisture from the leaves, cover the container with polythene. To keep it above the leaf blades, insert a 6-inch (15-centimetre) length of stick (as used for supporting indoor plants) at each of the four corners of the container, like a small tent.·

Watering is best done by immersing the base of the container for several minutes in lukewarm water rather than wetting the leaf blades. It is also important every few days to remove the polythene and to wipe it clear of any moisture. Wait half an hour before returning it, to give the leaves ventilation.

In a temperature of 60°F (16°C), the leaves will root in about 4 weeks but will take longer if the temperature falls below 56°F (14°C) and below this they may not root at all. Maintaining a suitable temperature is all-important, whilst fluorescent lighting will provide all the light that is necessary.

Along the whole length of the leaf stem inserted into the compost (or water), tiny plantlets will have formed. Some varieties root more freely than others and may produce as many as ten plantlets. When the leaves have formed a good bunch of roots, remove each leaf with care, so as not to damage them or the roots, and put them separately into 3-inch (7.5 centimetre) plastic pots containing the John Innes potting compost. If you wish to make up your own, the formula is:

> 7 parts sterilized fibrous loam
> 2 parts moist peat
> 2 parts silver sand

To each bushel of this mixture is added:
> 1½ oz hoof and horn meal
> ¾ oz sulphate of potash
> 1½ oz superphosphate

Normally, the John Innes potting compost contains 1 ounce of ground limestone but for Saintpaulias it is advisable to omit this. Whenever peat is used, make sure it is first made thoroughly moist. Peat absorbs large amounts of moisture which cannot be given later and if used too dry, the peat will take up moisture needed by the plants.

Growing on the Plants

When potting on the leaves, insert the petiole in the compost to almost its entire length, just leaving the base of the leaf blade clear of the compost. Stand the pots on trays under the artificial lighting and on a layer of moist pebbles. Maintain the room temperature at 60°F (16°C) and in 3 weeks a small tuft of plantlets will have formed around the base of the original leaf, like chicks around the mother hen. As soon as the plantlets are large enough to handle, remove the plant from the pot and split the crowns into separate plants and re-pot them using a similar compost. The potting compost should be porous and after potting, cover the surface of the compost with washed shingle. This will prevent the compost from coming into direct contact with the crown which should be kept free from soil and moisture throughout the life of the plant, otherwise it may damp off. For this reason it is best to water Saintpaulias from the base of the pot, by standing it in lukewarm water for several minutes daily, or around the side of the pot. It is advisable to water before midday so that the plant can use up any surplus moisture whilst the day temperature of 60°F (16°C) is maintained. At night the plants will take up little moisture, so that any surplus moisture should have been used up previously.

When potting on, do not use too big a pot. One of 3 inches (7.5 centimetres) diameter is suitable and do not forget to put a few crocks or small pebbles in the bottom before filling it with compost. Also, do not plant too firmly. The compost should be open and friable.

When potting, take care not to cover the heart or crown of the little plant. Just bury the roots, leaving the crown on top of the compost.

The best way of transplanting is to use a short piece of cane with the end made smooth. Then, holding the plant in the fingers of one hand and the cane in the other, make a small opening in the compost and drop in the roots.

During their first winter, water the plants as little as possible, just sufficient to keep them growing slowly and do not let the temperature fall below 56°F (14°C). In spring, they will need more moisture and during summer will make plenty of new leaves. By mid-August, the plants will be a mass of flower buds which are held on 4-inch (10-centimetre) stems just above the dark-green foliage. They are now ready to sell for they will bloom continuously from this time onwards. See your local florist in plenty of time and take a sample of your plants. When marketing, wrap each plant in its pot in a sheet of clean white paper and insert a small plastic label with the name on it. To begin with, do not grow more than six varieties, perhaps one or two doubles and one of each colour. The plants are not heavy and can be taken to shops in strong cardboard boxes holding six or eight plants.

Propagation by Division

African violets can also be propagated by division and this is a suitable way of removing old plants which may have lost their neat, compact habit and hence much of their charm. As they grow older, plants will form several new crowns, like primroses and when several years old are best divided. Remove the plant from its pot, gently shake away the soil from the roots and "tease" the plant apart to separate one crown from another. Then re-pot each plant into fresh compost after removing any dead or damaged leaves. Some growers plant several crowns attached to each other so as to obtain the maximum amount of bloom in the shortest possible time but, although they take longer to come into bloom from single crowns these will produce the most vigorous plants and so the most bloom. Neither will they need dividing again for several years.

Where the plants have formed a large amount of old roots, it will be advisable to cut away some of these with a sharp knife, to allow the most vigorous new roots to grow. These will be more active in searching for food and moisture than will old roots. In the same way, those crowns or offsets formed around the parent or central crown will be more vigorous when removed and re-potted than the parent crown which may have been deprived of food and moisture by its offsets. It may be that the stem from the central crown has grown too tall and weak and this should be cut back to the lowest pair of leaves when replanting. After re-planting the crowns, do not over-water for until the new roots form, the plants will be unable to absorb much moisture and if the soil is too wet, crown rot will set in and the plants will die back.

Growing from Seed

Baron Saint Paul-Illaine's original species, *Saintpaulia ionantha*, will grow true to type from seed, its unique deep purple-blue colouring ensuring that well-grown plants sell on sight. But you should also obtain the Grandiflora strain which bears larger flowers of greater colour intensity. Another reliable strain is Blue Fairy Tale which also comes true, the large flowers being of deepest blue with bright golden anthers. The new mixed colour hybrid strain, Fondant Creams, is also interesting.

The time to sow is in the early new year, or perhaps a few weeks earlier, using a propagator to maintain a temperature of 70°F (about 20°C) which ensures rapid and even germination. The Autogrow propagator is reasonably priced and it is possible to recoup its outlay from a single sowing and within twelve months for by sowing in midwinter and bringing on the plants under fluorescent lighting, the seedlings will be ready to transplant early in spring and the plants will begin to bloom in October.

The Autogrow is fitted with a thermostat which is set at the required temperature, whilst the heating element is rated at 15 watts per square foot. One light denotes that the mains is "on" whilst a second light switches "on" and "off" with the heating element. All electrical heating elements are moulded into the plastic base. The unit measures 30 inches by 16 inches to hold four seed trays and running costs work out to about 2 pence a day. The base is 3 inches deep but the polythene cover gives a total depth of 12 inches.

Seed is sown on the surface of a 2-inch (5-centimetre) deep mixture of silver sand and moist peat, or of vermiculite and moist peat; or use the John Innes sowing compost. Make the surface level and sow the tiny seeds thinly and evenly. Do not cover it. The seed must be fresh otherwise it may not germinate. Water it gently and keep the sowing medium just moist when, in about twenty days, the first seedlings will have appeared and others will do so at intervals for the next thirty days. Then lower the temperature to 60°F (16°C) which is maintained until the seedlings are ready to transplant. This is done when they have formed their fourth pair of leaves. They are lifted with a piece of smooth-ended cane or stick and transferred to plastic trays divided into compartments 2 inches (5 centimetres) square. Marketed under the name of Vacapots, the thin-walled plastic containers are detachable. The "pots" are filled with compost and one seedling is planted into each and watered in. The trays are then stood on shelves or on metal trays lit by fluorescent lighting and the young plants grown on. By early summer, in a temperature of 60°F (16°C) they will be ready to move to 3-inch (7.5-centimetre) pots containing the growing compost and in which they will come into bloom. The young plants should be removed from the Vacapots with little or no root disturbance and they will then grow away quickly in their new pots.

The growing of African violets for market is an all-year-round occupation and in this way full and profitable use can be made of a cellar. The work can be done under quite pleasant conditions, without the need for expensive transport to and from work and as long as watering is attended to, the growing of the plants will not take up the whole of one's time. If the plants are allowed to stand on damp pebbles, they will need the minimum of watering. Do so only when the compost becomes dry at the surface. In a temperature of 60°F (16°C) this will be only once or twice a week if the atmosphere is reasonably humid. In a cellar, this can be achieved by spraying the walls and floor at regular intervals and by carefully controlling the ventilation. It should be said that African violets will take no harm if the air temperature falls to as low as 50°F (10°C) but they will not produce flowers.

Pests and Diseases

As with all diseases, prevention is better than cure and if the plants are grown well from the start and in the correct compost which has a neutral or slightly acid reaction and are given the correct lighting and humidity, they will be strong and healthy, the foliage dark green, without blemishes, the habit neat and compact. In this condition, they will be rarely troubled with disease. In too high a temperature and under too dry conditions, the plants will grow lanky, the leaf stalks and flowering stems becoming too long so that the plants will have lost their natural charm, and be liable to attack by pests and disease. The leaves should be short and sturdy with the flowers appearing amongst them and just above.

It is also important that water is not allowed to splash on to the leaves for if it does not dry off quickly they may become blemished and decay may set in. It is of vital importance to prevent water coming into direct contact with the crown of the plant which will decay. If watering has to be done from above, give a little around the side of the pot and always use tepid water, warmed to the temperature of the room and use rain water if possible. African violets must not be allowed to grow in a saturated compost. If there is little or no evaporation of moisture from the compost, it means that the air temperature is too low or humidity too high. Tap the side of the pots and if there is a dull "thud", it will mean the compost is too wet. To confirm this, turn a plant upside down with the fingers of one hand held across the top of the soil ball and remove it from the pot. If excess moisture is seen around the side of the pot, it means the compost is too wet. Correct watering can only be learnt by experience but too little is better than giving too much.

Use new pots wherever possible (small plastic pots are inexpensive) but if using old pots, wash them first in soap and water and a reliable disinfectant. Thrips, which attack the leaves, feeding on the sap and reducing the plant's vitality, will be harboured in dirty pots and unsterilized compost. They cluster on the underside of the leaves as does that other troublesome pest, the cyclamen mite. Where present, the leaves will show signs of curling and the flower buds will fall. Routine dusting of the plants when young with flowers of sulphur will usually prevent an outbreak; or if their presence is suspected, spray with malathion, and repeat two weeks later. This will also kill aphids.

Mealy bugs, which also attack greenhouse-grown show auriculas, may attack the roots and stems of Saintpaulias and appear like tiny specks of cotton wool. They are readily seen and are exterminated by touching them with a child's paint brush dipped in methylated spirit. They are rarely troublesome if clean conditions are maintained.

Diseases are rare, for crown rot and bud drop are caused by unfavourable conditions and are not diseases in the accepted term whilst Ring Spot is caused by excess light on the leaves. This may be too much sunlight or an excess of artificial light.

Varieties

There are at least 2,000 known to growers for the plant readily lends itself to hybridizing but a small number are outstanding in their habit, colour and freedom of flowering and should form the base of any collection.

Beaming. The habit is compact, the leaves small and neat whilst the flowers are double and of clear bright pink.

Bicolor. A double, it is most unusual in that the top petals are deep mauve, the lower petals pale mauve.

Black Magic. The fully double flowers are royal blue with a bright-yellow eye and are held just above the broad, dark-green leaves.

Blue Boy. An older introduction, extremely free flowering, the bright purple-blue flowers having a striking gold centre.

Crown of Red. The leaves are of palest green and are more oval than round, whilst the semi-double blooms are of deepest crimson.

Delight. The flowers are double and of bright sky-blue, enhanced by the dark-green foliage.

Divine Song. It has double flowers of soft strawberry pink which are held above the foliage on strong stems.

Double Delight. The larger than usual double blooms are freely produced and are of a unique shade of French blue.

Gypsy Alma Girl. The foliage is bronzy-green, whilst the lavender blue flowers are borne in large trusses.

Hermione. A beautiful variety, its double white flowers having a tiny mauve centre whilst the leaves are of contrasting bottle green.

Lady Anne. The habit is neat and compact with the double blooms of rich lilac-mauve.

Lady Geneva. Of unique colouring, the large flowers being of an attractive shade of mauve-pink shaded with white.

Patricia. The leaves are serrated, the double blooms being of clear rose-pink.

Pink Ideal. Possibly the best double pink, the flowers being of a lovely shade of clear shell-pink.

Pink Pearl. The single pearl-pink flowers are produced with great freedom over many months.

Pink Rocket. A double pink of compact habit and freedom of flowering, the colour being deep rose.

Puck. A delightful plant of compact habit and bearing masses of flowers of rich blue.

Rainbow Rose. It is most attractive in that the large white blooms are double with frilled petals and heavily suffused with rose-pink.

Red Comet. A strong healthy grower bearing fully double blooms of rich wine-red.

Ruffled Queen. The deep-purple blooms are fully double and have an attractive ruffled edge to the petals.

Sailor's Delight. It quickly became a favourite when introduced for the double blooms are of a lovely shade of soft blue with the foliage attractively serrated.

Silver Lining. For long a standard variety for the fully double deep-blue flowers have an edging of silvery white to the petals to give an appearance of frilled lace.

Silver Tips. The double flowers are of a lovely shade of soft purple-mauve with a wire edge of silver to the petals.

Snow-white. Probably the best pure-white single for the flowers are produced in abundance above leaves of darkest green.

3

Mushrooms in the Cellar

The value of a cellar—Outlay and returns—How to grow mushrooms—Preparing the compost—Spawning and casing the beds—Bringing on the crop

Besides the use of a cellar for growing African violets, it will be equally profitable for growing mushrooms. I have written about it on many occasions for this is how I began my career in commercial horticulture and from early experiments in growing in a cellar and an old wash-house, built up a profitable business with more than 10,000 square feet under cultivation.

There is no better way of using an outhouse or cellar than filling it with mushroom beds for the temperature of a cellar, being below ground or partly so, is fairly constant the whole year round, being warmer in autumn and winter and cooler in summer than outside temperatures. This makes a cellar an ideal place to grow mushrooms for they thrive in a temperature of around 56°F (14°C) and this is an average cellar temperature. They will grow in much lower temperatures but in one less than 50°F (10°C) growth is slow. Should the beds become completely frozen, no damage is done but spawn growth is retarded. As soon as the temperature rises above 42°F (6°C), growth will begin again, though it will be slow. Rarely will the temperature of a cellar fall below 42°F (6°C) during winter and if a little artificial heat is used when the weather is really cold, it will be possible to have the beds in cropping, in a temperature of 50°–52°F (10°–11°C) throughout the winter and this is the time of year when mushrooms make most money. During summer they have to compete with soft fruits, and cooks used to say that they did not wish to have mushrooms in the kitchen until St Leger Day, early in September.

In summer, the temperature of a cellar will be lower than the air outside and by using a cooling fan, it can be reduced still further, so that except when the weather is really warm, the cellar temperature should not rise above 65°F (18°C). In this warmth the crop will come on quickly and the beds must be picked over every day, but in higher temperatures the mushrooms grow thin and lose moisture all the time. This reduces their weight and the weight of the crop and so makes them less profitable, whilst thin-stalked mushrooms are never popular. The next best place to a cellar is a stone or brick-built outhouse or garage which can be put to more profitable use than keeping a car in it. A building of stone or brick will also keep fairly cool in summer and is warm in winter with just a little help from artificial heating if the electric supply is on hand. Tubular heaters which are impervious to moisture are suitable.

With many an old house, the cellar is three-parts below ground and there is an opening, originally for coal deliveries but now for mushroom compost, whilst some cellars have an opening window just above ground level. This will give light for working amongst the beds and provide ventilation but mushrooms grow best in total darkness which gives a cellar additional value. They grow well in diffused light but sunlight is detrimental for it dries out the beds and will quickly bring the crop to an end when otherwise it would have continued for weeks, perhaps months. Nor do mushrooms like excessive humidity. Stagnant air conditions are not to be encouraged. The atmosphere of a mushroom house should be sweet and fresh, for as little as 5 per cent carbon dioxide will retard spawn growth. Excess watering of the compost will also kill the spawn. More mushroom beds are spoilt by giving too much moisture than for any other reason. Always keep the beds on the dry side for if too dry the crop will be retarded although little harm will be done. When the beds are given a little more water, mushrooms will appear again. The biggest crops of outdoor mushrooms always follow a hot dry summer, never a wet one. The autumn dews on dry ground are all that is required for the growing spawn to produce mushrooms which are the fruit of the mycelium. From the gills beneath the caps, the spores are released and are grown on under scientifically controlled conditions to produce the modern pure culture spawn which now assures a clean, heavy crop if the compost is correctly prepared and correct temperature and humidity is maintained.

Under most large old houses, there are two cellars, side by

side, one used for coal and wood, the other for wine. Now, it is rare for either to be used for their intended purpose but by growing mushrooms in them, it is possible to ensure continuous supplies which is what greengrocers and supermarkets require to satisfy their customers. Long breaks in the supply will force them to look elsewhere. If one room is filled with beds in early August, the mushrooms will appear early in September and continue until Christmas. Then if a second room is put down early in November, another crop will be ready in January, though it may be necessary to use a little artificial heat at this time to keep the beds cropping. These beds will crop until early summer when new beds put down in the first room can be made to produce another crop. The work is not arduous and is of absorbing interest. Though it can be a full-time occupation or just a hobby, it is no more demanding of one's time than growing any other crop and besides being profitable, mushrooms can be used in so many ways in the kitchen.

Outlay and Returns

For the small outlay involved there must be few crops capable of making such handsome returns. In addition, few things apart from winning the football pools will recoup the outlay in so short a time. It will take three weeks to prepare the compost in which the spawn will grow and another three weeks will elapse before the first pin-head mushrooms appear. The first will then be ready to pick in another 7–10 days, depending on temperature, so that there should be returns in about 50 days and a good first "flush" will usually recoup the whole of one's outlay. This does not include the cost of the wooden boxes or shelves on which the mushrooms are grown. What returns to expect can be calculated from each 100 square feet of bed space. Two bales of wheat straw would be necessary for this area (though larger quantities are more easily prepared); plus 2 pounds of activator to break down the straw and which is prepared to a special formula for mushroom composts, Adco "M" being suitable; and 3 cartons of pure culture spawn for every 100 square feet of bed. The total cost would be about £10. Only wheat straw is used for it has a calose on which the spawn "runs" and as it does so, feeds on the cellulose and lignin in the straw. Also present is a carbohydrate called xylan which ensures heavy mycelium growth. The mycelium or spawn threads will grow out from the spawn pieces as soon as planted and will eventually permeate the entire bed (compost) and a good spawn run is essential for a profitable crop.

With a little practice, it is possible to average one pound of mushrooms per square foot of bed and a good crop will produce anything up to two pounds. Even one pound per square foot at present prices will be worth £100 retail or about £75 if selling through a greengrocer. Thus if there is a cellar or shed capable of accommodating 240–250 square feet and two crops a year can be obtained, the return at wholesale prices would be about £400 or £8 a week. If two rooms (or perhaps a cellar and a garage or barn) were available, the income would be doubled, this from an area of 1000 square feet on which the total outlay would be about £100. By selling some of the produce retail to friends and neighbours, it will be possible to increase one's income to about £20 a week, and a housewife could comfortably manage an area of 1000 square feet in her limited time.

How to Grow Mushrooms

The beds can be made up directly on the ground though many more square feet can be grown if tiers or shelves are arranged around the walls of a cellar or shed. Use 3 inch by 3 inch timber for the uprights and back and front supports as the shelves have to take a considerable weight of compost and soil. Four-inch (10-centimetre) boards should be fixed along the front of each shelf to retain the compost and for the shelves, use galvanized flat iron sheets which are placed over strong wooden boards about 3 inches (7.5 centimetres) apart. About 18 inches should be allowed between each shelf or tier whilst the shelves should be no more than 2 feet 6 inches deep (from the front to the wall) to enable picking to be done right to the back. The number of shelves will be determined by the height of the room. If it is 10 feet high, then at 18 inches apart and with the lowest tier 12 inches (30 centi-metres) above ground level, also allowing about 8 inches (20 centimetres) for the depth of side boards and timbers, four shelves could be erected. Thus, against a wall 12 feet long, 120 square feet of shelf space could be obtained and with a wall on either side, an area of 240 square feet would be available. A cellar 9 or 10 feet wide would allow room at the centre for filling and tending to shelf beds.

Mushrooms growing in trays

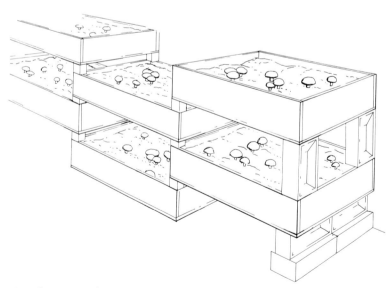

Another way of growing mushrooms in boxes which can be stacked
around the walls of a shed or cellar

Another way of increasing the area of a cellar or garage is to build up in tiers or rows a number of wooden fish boxes. These are strongly made and enable 4–5 square feet of mushroom bed to be grown in each. They are obtainable from timber merchants in Hull or Grimsby who make them to a standard size for fish merchants and cost about £2 each. The boxes are 6 inches (15 centimetres) deep and about 48 will provide an area of about 240 square feet. They can be stacked around the walls but should have been treated with Cuprinol or another wood preservative before taking them indoors. The boxes are placed alternately, one above another, a brick being used to support those boxes at either end of the row whilst the boxes rest on each other. There is sufficient depth above each box to allow for picking the mushrooms. They are taken inside before filling with compost.

Preparing the Compost

Possibly the best time to begin operations is early August and as artificially prepared compost has no unpleasant smell, it can be prepared inside, in a cellar or garage or outside in a small court-yard, possibly close to where the mushrooms are to be grown. Do not attempt to prepare less than two bales of straw for less than this quantity will not heat up correctly and the straw will not break down so that only a very light crop will result.

Before beginning the composting, first make the straw thoroughly moist. Like peat, straw will take up large amounts of water before it becomes thoroughly moist and it is advisable to open up the bales loosely and to allow the rains to penetrate, so obtain the straw at least three or four weeks before required. In dry weather, use a hose or watering-can or pour in water from a bucket. This must be done outside so that any excess moisture can drain away. When the straw is quite wet, shake it out and move it inside for its preparation will now begin.

Spread out a layer 6 inches (15 centimetres) deep over an area of about 20 square feet (4 feet by 5 feet). The heap is best made in a corner formed by two walls where it can be kept more compact and if outdoors, it will be protected from winds which will dry out the straw. The heap should be built up to at least 5 feet (1.5 metres) high, preferably 6–7 feet (2 metres) when it will generate considerable heat. This is necessary for the thorough preparation of the compost and also to kill any pests. If possible, keep the straw away from soil from the time it arrives for soil contains the spores of the dreaded Mycogone perniciosa disease which causes the mushrooms to become distorted and to ooze an unpleasantly smelling liquid, hence its name of "Bubbles" disease. For this reason, soil that has not been sterilized should never be used to "case" the beds. This is a term used when the beds are covered with an inch of sterilized loam or with peat and chalk. Into this, the mycelium will run and fuse together, thereby creating the fruiting body, the mushroom. The beds cannot crop until the casing is on.

But first the preparation of the straw. After spreading out a 6-inch (15-centimetre) layer, sprinkle over it some of the activator. This will cause the straw to heat up and break down and will transform the straw into food for the mushroom to feed on. A well-prepared bed should produce mushrooms for at least three months, depending upon how well the compost is prepared and upon prevailing temperatures. If one has a small quantity of dry pigeon or poultry manure available, sprinkle some of this over it as well for it will give the compost "body" and will cause the straw to generate more heat. Then add another layer of straw and more activator and so on until the straw is used up. Keep a little of the activator to use when the straw is first turned. This is done when it can be seen that the heap is generating some heat and will be steaming at the top. If doing the composting outdoors, cover the heap with sacking after leaving the top slightly dome-shaped. This will enable excess rain water to drain off and the sacking will help the heap to retain its heat.

After about a week, the temperature of the heap will reach 50°C (120°F). This will initiate bacterial activity which will cause the straw to break down when it turns a rich brown and has the wholesome smell of mushrooms. After another day or two, the heap will be ready to turn. This means shaking out the straw and the ingredients as it is rebuilt into another heap nearby. This will ensure that the ingredients are thoroughly mixed together whilst more air (oxygen) can reach to all parts, thus giving rise to greater bacterial activity, thereby enabling the straw to be cured more quickly. If there are any dry areas, give more water and sprinkle in a little more activator. If readily obtainable from a builder's merchant, at this stage sprinkle in as the heap is turned a small amount of gypsum, which is pink plaster of Paris, used in hospitals to set broken limbs. Used at the rate of about 7lbs for every 2 bales of wheat straw, this will prevent the compost becoming heavy and sticky when it will set like lard in the beds as it goes cold. This will cause the growing spawn to be deprived of vital oxygen without which it will not grow. The introduction of gypsum (which is quite inexpensive) in the mid-1930s, at about the same time as pure culture spawn, revolutionized commercial mushroom growing everywhere. When gypsum has been used, the compost will be spongy, with the straw short and of a rich brown colour. When ready to make up into the beds, a large handful should be taken up and twisted in the hands when the straw should break easily, leaving the hands moist but no large amounts of water should exude. This condition will usually be reached after three turns, over a period of 3–4 weeks from the time the heap is first made up. The second and third turns are given after about 6–7 days for by then the compost will be generating considerable heat.

No more turns should be given unless the straw is still long for to over-compost will cause the straw to lose much of its heat and food value and the crop will be short-lived. There is just the right time to put down the beds and this is only determined by experience. Like making a sponge cake, in the kitchen, it may take two or three "goes" to get it just right when the composted straw can be expected to produce mushrooms for at least 12 weeks and bear one pound per square foot. If composting outside, it is advisable to make the last turn indoors, where the beds are to be made up, for this will protect the compost from heavy rain whilst it will better retain its heat when the beds are made up. It is shaken out on to the shelves or into the boxes and to do this, and also to turn the heap during the preparation of the compost, use a manure fork which facilitates the task. Such a fork may be picked up for a small sum at a country sale but it will be worthwhile investing in a new one if it is intended to take up mushroom growing seriously. One should also contact an established grower and ask if one might pay him or her a visit with a view to learning something about mushroom culture. Much can be learnt about the preparation of the compost and cleanliness necessary and there are some who will pass on this information.

When bedding down the compost, press it down around the sides of the boxes and in the corners, using a brick or thick piece of wood to do so. There should be a 6-inch (15-centimetre) depth

A brick is used to press the compost firm

of compost to produce a good crop and nothing is gained by making it deeper but if less deep, it may dry out too quickly in warm weather and the crop will come to a premature end.

Spawning and Casing the Beds

When all the compost is used up, the spawn is planted. Dry spawn comes in cylinders, one of which will spawn about 30 square feet of bed, so order 3 cartons for every 100 square feet. As it will keep for several years, obtain it in plenty of time for it must be on hand exactly when required. This will be several hours after making up the beds, when their temperature will have dropped to around 68°–70°F (20°C).

Each carton is broken up into pieces of the size of a walnut and is pressed into the compost about 1 inch (2.5 centimetres) deep and 6 inches (15 centimetres) apart. Cover it by pressing some compost over the top and use up all the bits for every particle of spawn will grow and will begin to do so at once. In an air temperature of around 60°F (15°C), the mycelium will have permeated the compost within 3–4 weeks. The dark-brown compost will then be white with spawn growth and it will have a

Inserting the spawn in the compost

distinct mushroom smell. This condition signifies that all is well and that a good crop can be expected. But there will be no mushrooms until the beds are covered with 1 inch (2.5 centimetres) of sterilized soil; or if this is unobtainable, use a mixture of crushed chalk (in small pieces about pea or pebble size) and moist peat. Never use garden soil for it will be full of disease spores. Spread the casing materials over the compost so that the beds are covered to an even depth and from now on, keep the casing slightly moist but not wet. Never at any time should water be allowed to percolate through the casing on to the compost beneath it for too much moisture will kill the growing spawn.

Bringing on the Crop

Give the beds plenty of fresh air but not draughts and in about 2 weeks after casing, the first tiny pin-head mushrooms will appear, first in a circle or clump above the place where each piece of spawn was inserted. It will take 6–7 days before the mushrooms reach saleable size but see your greengrocer or insert a small advertisement in the local newspaper as soon as the tiny mushrooms appear. When reaching the large button stage, just

Mushrooms in the last stage of development

before the caps begin to open flat and when the gills on the underside are of flesh pink colouring, they are removed. Often several will grow from a central stem from which they are snapped off. Others grow separately and these are twisted from the bed. Cut away the lower portion of the stem before placing the mushrooms on trays or in shallow boxes, cap downwards. The small mushrooms are left on the beds to mature and when the first full flush has been removed, look over the beds with a sharp knife and lift out any stems or brown mushrooms, filling in the holes with more of the casing material and into this the spawn will run. Then lightly water the beds to bring on another flush. Mushrooms grow in flushes, at intervals of about a fortnight and as each flush matures, the beds need slightly more water though never so much as to reach the compost below the casing. Always err on the side of dryness.

It is also necessary to keep the beds clear of phorid and sciarid flies which lay their eggs in the compost from the time the beds are made up. When the grubs hatch out, they tunnel up the stalks and into the caps, making them unsaleable. They also feed on the growing mycelium, thus reducing the crop. They can be exter-

The author with a box of mushrooms which have been cropped for
three months in a cellar

minated and the beds kept clean of pests by dusting them once each week from the time the beds are made up with pyrethrum powder. It is non-poisonous and is applied by a bellows. Quite inexpensive, the powder is obtainable from Messrs W. Darlington & Sons Ltd, of Angmering-on-Sea, Sussex, who also supply pure culture spawn and other mushroom growing requirements.

Mushrooms are marketed in 4-lb baskets or in ½-lb and 1-lb punnets covered with a piece of cellophane. Take care when watering not to splash soil on to the snow-white caps and do not dirty them with the fingers when picking. Their whiteness is their main attraction for the buyer and as they lose weight all the time, they must be marketed as soon as possible after picking. If selling to greengrocers and supermarkets, pick the mushrooms between 7 and 8 a.m. and have them with the retailer by 9 a.m. or as soon as the shop opens its doors. Also, tell the retailer how many more you will have for later that day if the demand is brisk or for the morrow so that he (or she) will not order elsewhere. The one drawback with mushrooms is that they are highly perishable, like strawberries, and must be marketed the moment they are ready (mature). Even to delay for several hours will be for the crop to deteriorate on the beds, the mushrooms opening flat before turning brown and losing weight. They will then be worth much less than if marketed at their best.

The utmost cleanliness is necessary at all times. When the crop has finished after about 12 weeks, and this will depend upon temperatures and the way in which the compost was prepared, clear the boxes (or shelves) of compost which is best done by filling strong paper sacks and selling it to local gardeners for it has considerable manurial value. Then carry out the boxes or the galvanized sheets used for shelf beds and wash in a reliable disinfectant before replacing them for a new crop. During this time fresh compost will be prepared.

4

King of Begonias

Its introduction—Cultural requirements—Propagation—
Growing on the plants—Varieties

At one time the Rex begonia grew in every Victorian home, usually
near the aspidistra for both enjoy similar conditions, the half
light of a heavily curtained room and a dry atmosphere; but there
is no need to have central heating to grow Begonia rex, one of the
most beautiful and accommodating plants ever introduced, of
easy culture and absorbing interest. Of all indoor plants it is one
of the easiest to manage. The plants can be left for weeks without
attention if need be and even if they die back altogether, will
come again when watering is resumed. Their leaf shape, metallic
colourings and diverse markings give them a beauty not to be
found in other house plants.

Begonia rex was first observed growing in northern India,
almost at the foot of the Himalayas in about 1860. Shortly after,
just one plant arrived at the nursery of John Simmons in London
and together with a collection of orchids, he took the plant to be
sold at Steven's Auction Rooms. Attending the sale was one Jean
Linden, a nurseryman of Brussels and a wealthy grower of exotic
plants which were then being grown in their thousands to
decorate the large conservatories being built on to the homes of
those who had made fortunes during the early days of the indus-
trial revolution. It was not realized at the time that this begonia
would grow as well in the half light of a back-street terraced
house cared for by a housewife as it would in a heated conservatory attended by a professional gardener, but it caused a
sensation when auctioned and was purchased by Linden, in
competition with other continental bidders for a sum which
was the equivalent of 10,000 francs. He was on to a winner and so
easily did it propagate that he was able to introduce plants to

Rex begonia, Iron Cross

commerce within 18 months. On account of its great beauty, he named the plant King of Begonias, Begonia rex. Within a year of his introducing it, Linden earned by his business foresight over half a million francs for his firm and his plants went out to all parts of the western world. He next began crossing his original plant with *Begonia xanthina pictafolia* with its beautifully silvered leaves and so laid the foundation of the Rex hybrids we know today, plants of such easy culture that they can be grown and propagated by any housewife working at home with only limited time on her hands.

The next step was to cross Linden's hybrids with *Begonia decora* which imparted its rich colourings of bronze, pink, purple and crimson to the leaves and which gave the Rex begonia a new popularity in Edwardian times. By then, it was also realized that the plants would grow well in the home, that all they required was a frost-free room and not the great heat of a conservatory. And they were so easily managed that a child could see to them after school.

During Edwardian times, the plants were also used for summer bedding in the gardens of the wealthy, for the silver leaves and their strikingly handsome markings blended to perfection with the Paul Crampel geranium, another favourite of Edwardian gardens with its blooms of pillar-box red. In recent years the Rex begonias have fallen from favour for it is thought that their exotic appearance makes it necessary to grow them in considerable heat and that they are difficult to manage when in fact, they are the easiest of plants.

Cultural Requirements

They require a frost-free room and will grow well in a temperature of 50°F (10°C) which is provided in most homes, but a lower temperature may cause an outbreak of mildew. Much in their favour is their ability to recover from almost total neglect. Geraniums will drop their leaves and will cease to bloom but will recover when watered and taken in hand again, whilst African violets will never recover from neglect, but the Rex begonia will completely revive and continue to grow as if nothing has happened. Once when away from home for an intended few days and taken ill, I had to spend nearly a month in hospital and all the time I thought of my Rex begonia plants dying without a sip of water. Upon my return home, the plants did indeed appear past redemption and although the leaves still remained attached to the plants, they were so limp that they lay all around the pots whilst the compost was as dry as dust. My first reaction was that the plants were too far gone to do anything with but I thought of putting them in the bath for several hours, about twenty at a time and immersing the pots, almost to the rim, in cold water. By evening, after eight or nine hours, the first batch had recovered entirely, as if they had never been left unattended and they were replaced by another twenty or so which were left overnight. By morning, these too had completely recovered and within 48 hours of returning home, the entire collection appeared exactly as I had left them. They are plants which will look after themselves if one has to be away from home for any length of time. When this happens, stand the pots in a bowl of water and place them in diffused light. Indeed, the plants are more beautiful in the home than in the greenhouse for strong sunlight will bleach the leaves and the amazing colourings and markings will become less intense. If growing in a greenhouse in summer, place the plants under the bench or shade the glass. Another method is to tack sheets of brown paper on the inside, if the greenhouse is of wooden construction. A plant will be happy in its 5-inch pot for several years, with the compost only occasionally topped with fresh compost and they require only sufficient moisture to keep them growing. They are re-potted every third year. And all the time they will provide a constant supply of new leaves to propagate. Keeping the plants in diffused light will reduce the need for watering which in winter will perhaps be necessary only once each week, twice in summer, though in the dry atmosphere of central heating, the compost will dry out more quickly. The best method of watering established plants is to stand the pots in 2 inches of water in the kitchen sink and leave them an hour to enjoy a long drink. At the same time spray the foliage, shaking off the surplus moisture when returning the plants to the living-room. It is not advisable to do this in winter if the house has no central heating.

It is entirely for their handsome foliage that the Rex begonia is grown. It is an evergreen and a well-grown plant will continue to produce new leaves for years. It is therefore advisable to remove the older leaves when there is overcrowding and they begin to lose their brilliance, though this will not be necessary when regularly removing the leaves for propagation. One of the best ways of displaying the plants in the home is to suspend them from a wall in a wrought-iron bracket, capable of holding three plants or one holding individual plants. The size of the pot in which they grow will control the vigour of the plants though a few possess extra natural vigour whilst some, such as Cotswold and Green Velvet, are of compact habit and are usually grown in a pot of 4-inch (10-centimetre) diameter. These compact varieties are suitable plants for a windowbox facing west or north-west. I have seen them producing their brilliant leaf-colourings in the coldest and wettest of summers, buffeted by strong winds and saturated by heavy rain, yet completely untroubled and defying their description of "stove-house" plants as given in the garden books of a century ago. They should be taken indoors early in October as frost will damage the plants.

A good way of keeping stock plants is to grow them outdoors in summer in window boxes, long wooden boxes placed on a terrace or verandah or around the side of a courtyard which may be attached to a terrace house and is usually surrounded by a high wall. The plants can be taken indoors early October and placed on trays on a sideboard in the living-room or on window ledges away from the direct rays of the sun, though the winter sunshine will cause them little trouble.

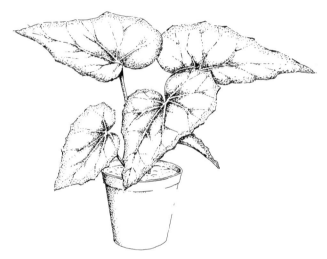

A young Rex begonia plant

Rex begonia leaves are about 8 inches (20 centimetres) long and are about 5 inches (12.5 centimetres) across at the widest part, which is at the point where the leaf stalk is attached to the blade. The leaves are almost triangular in shape, terminating to a point. Some have serrated edges and all have a metallic lustre which is especially pronounced with the silver-leaf varieties. Some are broader than others, some longer and narrower, whilst a well-grown plant at two years old will measure from 12–20 inches (30–50 centimetres) across depending upon the vigour of the variety and size of pot in which it is growing.

Propagation

Unlike the large flowering begonias, the plants form a rhizomatous root not a tuber. These roots are thick and fleshy and tend to grow out of the soil when they become crowded in the pots. When this happens, remove the plants from the pots and with a sharp knife, cut the rhizomes or fleshy roots, into small sections, each with a leaf. This can be done in alternate years and is a reliable way of increasing the stock. But a quicker way is to do this by leaf propagation. You will need a window or two (but not one facing south for in summer the sun will be too hot) and a number of plastic seed boxes or wide pots as used for bulb culture. One or two leaves are removed from each plant so as not to deprive them of too many at one time and those selected should be of average size, neither too old (large) nor too young (small).

Remove the leaves close to the rhizome using a sharp knife to do so, then remove the stem (leaf stalk) close to the point of contact with the leaf blade. Shallow boxes or pans should be filled with a mixture of moist peat and sand made firm and quite level. If a seed box (a kipper box will do) is used, three leaves can be rooted. Place each one on the surface of the compost with the underside of the leaves uppermost. Then take a sharp penknife and holding the leaf firmly with the fingers of one hand, make a series of short cuts across the veins of the leaf, about a dozen on each leaf, spacing them about 1 inch (2.5 centimetres) apart. Make the cuts just below the points at which the side veins join the main arteries, then turn the leaves over, with the underside downwards and lay them on the surface of the moist compost. They are held in place with the under surface in contact with the compost, by placing small pebbles on top of the leaves.

Leaf propagation can be carried out at any time but spring and early summer is the most reliable time, when temperatures are around 60°F (15°C) which is right for their rooting and the plants will then be established by late autumn. But if this degree of warmth can be maintained throughout the year, propagation can be done at any time.

To prevent the compost from drying out too quickly, fix plastic sheets over the boxes and if in sunlight (which should be avoided if possible) place brown paper over the plastic whenever the midday sun is at its fiercest. Should the compost dry out, rooting

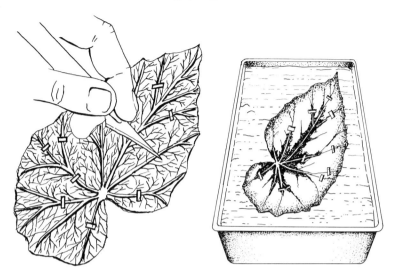

Nicking the underside of a Rex begonia leaf (*left*), and (*right*) the leaf turned upside down and placed on a layer of compost to root and form plants where the cuts were made

will not take place. It is advisable to syringe the leaves on alternate days to encourage quicker rooting. Indeed, humidity must be maintained at all times during the propagation period for if conditions are too dry when rooting has taken place, the tiny rootlets will shrivel and die.

About a month after the cuts were made in the leaf veins, small bulbils will appear from the places where this was done and tiny shoots or plantlets will then appear. Keep the surface of the compost comfortably moist and remove the pebbles from the leaves. The remainder of the leaves will now quickly decay, leaving behind the tiny plantlets which are lifted from the compost as soon as they are large enough to handle. Do not leave them too long undisturbed for if the compost used in their rooting was a mixture of sand and peat it will be almost devoid of plant food and will be unable to sustain the plants for much longer.

Growing on the Plants

The plantlets are now moved to 2-inch (5-centimetre) pots containing the John Innes potting compost. With a dibber, make a small hole in the surface of the compost and drop in the roots.

Then carefully cover them with compost and make firm before watering them in. Stand the plants in the half light and no artificial heat will be necessary if propagation took place in April or May. By early September, the plants will be ready to move to 5-inch (12.5 centimetre) pots containing fresh John Innes potting compost (obtainable from garden shops) or one made to this formula:

> 3 parts fibrous turf loam
> 1 part decayed manure
> 1 part moist peat
> 1 part grit or coarse sand.

The loam should either be freshly dug pasture loam or the soil should be sterilized. Do not use soil from a town garden which most likely will be full of weed and disease spores. And do not use artificial fertilizers, especially of a nitrogenous nature, which will cause the leaves to grow unduly large and coarse.

The best form of plant food is old mushroom-bed compost which will have broken down to a mould-like consistency and is ideal for most pot plants. Otherwise use well-decayed cow manure which is fairly dry and broken down. Do not omit the grit. Additional quantities may be included in the John Innes potting compost for Rex begonias enjoy an "Open", gritty compost from which surplus moisture can rapidly drain and which suits the growth of the rhizomatous roots. For the same reason use an earthenware pot for the stock plants if obtainable, as the roots love to be in contact with the side, but these pots are now becoming difficult to find. If smooth plastic pots are used, then extra grit in the compost is essential.

When propagating from the rhizomes and replanting, set the rhizome almost in a horizontal position just below the surface of the compost and leave the upper portion of the rhizome uncovered by the compost. Gently press the compost round the rhizome and water in. It will be found that the roots tend to grow out horizontally, making for the side of the pot and within a year will have protruded over the side, sometimes by several inches. Do not break them off by careless handling of the plants and remember to keep the plants away from the sunlight until established in the pots, though from mid-October until the end of March the sun will not affect them. Rex begonias, however, do prefer the partial shade of a living-room for excessive sunlight will take the colouring from the leaves.

The best way to water the plants is to stand them in several inches of water in the kitchen sink and let them drink for an hour. In summer, occasionally syringe the foliage but not in winter as the water may take too long to dry off and will cause brown markings to appear on the leaves.

When the leaves become old, usually after about two years, the edges will begin to curl and the rich markings to fade. They should then be removed, perhaps one from each plant, snipping off the stems close to the rhizome. Using the leaves for propagation will usually prevent any leaves becoming too old and will maintain a nicely balanced plant. New leaves will soon take the place of those removed.

Potting on to larger-size pots will build up a plant of large proportions and amazing beauty but do not use too big a pot until the plants are well established. An occasional top dressing will maintain the vigour of the plants and reduce the need for re-potting. This is done once every two or three years and presents little difficulty. Remove the soil ball from the pot and transfer it to a slightly larger pot containing freshly prepared compost. Do not disturb the roots by breaking up the soil ball and when re-potting, ensure that the horizontal rhizomes are only half covered with the new compost.

Plants in 5-inch (12.5-centimetre) pots, which is the best-selling size, will make about 75p–80p from the florists and will sell for £1.20 or so. With their handsome leaf markings they sell on sight and are one of the easiest of indoor plants to manage and one of the most beautiful. The blooms are rarely produced and there is no petal drop to cause a nuisance. It is the leaves that provide the beauty.

Take them to your local florist in cardboard boxes holding about six plants, each of which is wrapped in clean white paper to protect the leaves from bruising in the box. If you can add a label to each, bearing the plant's name, the customer will appreciate this information.

You can begin with half a dozen varieties of widely different markings and include perhaps two of each of three varieties in each box sold. Some will be more popular than others and you will soon discover which these are. Wherever possible, maintain a regular supply of saleable plants so that the florist can rely on plants being usually available. The supermarkets too will take them up. The plants present no trouble to the florist for they need little water and there are no fading flowers to spoil the display if the plants (due to holidays or bad weather) do not sell immediately. The plants are ideal for display in banks, hotels and shops and these will be your customers too.

Varieties

There are many outstanding varieties, all possessing individual beauty but some of the most striking are:

Cotswold. Of compact habit, it is a symphony in green, like the Cotswolds in summer and well named; the pale silvery-green leaves have deeper-green markings.

Etna. A striking variety of intense brilliance, the crimson-brown leaves being splashed with silver and pink. It is a plant of compact habit.

Everest. The large silver leaves have contrasting veins of deepest green.

Fireflush. A most interesting variety in that the bright mid-green leaves are covered with red hairs; like the reflection from a coal fire.

Gloire des Ardennes. Raised in France it is a large leaf variety of a uniform crimson colouring.

Glory of St Albans. A chance seedling raised by the famous orchid growers, Messrs Sanders of St Albans towards the end of the last century; it is still obtainable and is a plant of considerable beauty. The leaves are bright rose-red, margined with olive green and with a small patch of olive green at the centre of each leaf.

Green Velvet. Of compact habit, the deeply indented leaves are of darkest green with velvet-black markings.

Haldon. Striking in that the leaves alternate in broad bands of light and dark green.

Helene Temple. The neatly formed leaves are of rich velvet-green with blotches of silver and the whole leaf covered with purple hairs to make it one of the most beautiful of all the Rex hybrids.

Himalaya. The large pale-green leaves are heavily splashed with silver which gives the plant a brilliant sheen.

La Perle de Mortefontain. This striking variety has bright reddish-pink leaves, shaded crimson at the edges.

Mountain Stream. Of compact habit, the glittering leaves are of metallic silver, shaded with pink and pale green.

Remilly. Its large silver leaves have a flush of pale mauve.

Rougemont. The large handsome leaves are of rich cherry-red with an attractive pink and brown border.

Vesuvius. A plant of vigorous habit, the large crimson-brown leaves are splashed with shades of pink.

Wallingbrook. A robust grower, its large leaves have a triple zone of various shades of green and with a dark-green blotch at the centre.

Woodbury. The leaves are deep purple with unusual black spots along the prominent veins.

5

Scented-leaf Geraniums

Their introduction—Cultural requirements—Propagation
—Growing on the plants—Species and varieties

The scented-leaf geraniums (really pelargoniums) are amongst the most easily managed of all indoor plants and are amongst the most interesting. Happy in the diffused light of a cottage window, where they have been grown for centuries, often in the same pot, the plants are equally at home in the half light of a city flat or a Victorian town house for although they are plants of sun-drenched South Africa, especially Cape Province, and tolerant of intense sunlight, they are just as accommodating in partial shade, as happy in the home as in the greenhouse or garden room. They were discovered by travellers to South Africa early in the seventeenth century and plants first reached England during the reign of Charles I though for two hundred years they remained comparatively neglected, only to be found in cottage windows. Even when the large flowered geraniums came to be grown in the conservatories of wealthy industrialists in Victorian times, the scented-leaf geraniums found no place in the heated glass structures though they were to be found in some homes whilst still beautifying the window sills of the humble cottage. And what interesting plants they are with their many leaf variations and diverse scents which they release when the leaves are lightly pressed between the fingers. The scents are refreshing rather than cloying, some smelling of orange, others of lemon. From the leaves of *Pelargonium capitatum* "attar of rose" is made and used to adulterate the concentrated rose perfumes of Bulgaria where the finest attar is made. When pressed, the leaf of *Pelargonium capitatum* releases a distinct rose scent, the oil from which is twice as powerful as that obtained from rose flowers. The same substance, geraniol, found in attar of roses, is also

Left *Pelargonium crispum variegatum*

Below *Pelargonium tomentosum*

present in the rose-leaf geranium, in which it is stored in cells. The powerful scent found in leaves is due to evaporation of moisture from the cells as the leaf ages, leaving behind the essential oil in concentrated form. This is why leaf odours are more persistent than the scents of flowers. There are few plants with scented flowers in hot, arid countries but many have scented leaves. By releasing an oily vapour from the foliage, the plants are able to protect themselves from the intense heat, the vapour covering the plants in a cloudlike barrier which also protects them from excessive moisture evaporation. The thickness of the leaves of several species of pelargonium also enables the plants to store up moisture which will carry them through a long period of drought and with some species, this is carried a step further, as with the peppermint-scented *P. tomentosum* whose leaves are covered in downy hairs which gives them a velvet-like appearance and additional protection from heat and moisture evaporation.

Whilst all the scented-leaf geraniums are powerfully scented when pressed, they are also of diverse sizes, shapes and markings. The habit of the plants also varies greatly. With *P. crispum variegatum* which releases a delicious lemon scent when pressed, the leaves are small with attractively waved edges and are pale green with a margin of gold. The habit too is also pyramidal. With *P. filicifolium*, the leaves are considerably dissected, whilst those of *P. tomentosum* are broad and flat and held on a long footstalk. The covering of downy hairs gives them a thick flannel-like feeling when touched.

Cultural Requirements

With but one or two exceptions, the flowers these plants produce are insignificant but the great beauty of the leaves and their many scents gives them an interest not to be found in other indoor plants. In addition their ease of culture enables them to be grown by almost anyone, almost anywhere. All they require is a frost-free room. Along the south coast of England and on the south-western side of Scotland, they can be grown outdoors with the expectation that they will survive all but the severest of winters. Elsewhere, they should be housed in winter in the home or in a garden room where they will be happy in a temperature which does not fall below 50°F (10°C) nor rise above 62°F (16°C). And like

Pelargonium filicifolium. It has grey-green foliage with a cream-white margin

Begonia rex, they require the minimum of moisture, especially in winter when they need watering only about once in three weeks. For this reason, the plants can be left for some little time without attention if one has to be away from home. In summer, they can be grown in their pots on a terrace or verandah and moved indoors in October when they will grow well in almost any place in the home. The Victorians would have a few large plants growing in pots at the side of stairs (fastened to the bannister rails), so that those wearing long clothes would brush against the leaves causing them to release their scent which is pungent and refreshing. A few leaves, removed with care and dried, make a pleasing addition to a *pot-pourri* or they may be placed in muslin bags to put under the pillow case or in drawers amongst clothes, those of lemon scent being most refreshing.

They also have other uses: the leaves of *P. tomentosum* can be used to make a delicious peppermint jelly to serve with meats and from the leaves of *P. odoratissimum*, an apple-tasting conserve can be made.

The plants can be grown in the home or in a garden room. They can be propagated by "striking" (rooting) the cuttings in pots in the windows of a room where for example in the large window of a Victorian house as many as a dozen 5-inch (12.5-centimetre) pots can be placed on small squares of wood to prevent damaging the paint. There should be no fear of water percolating from the base for throughout their life, the plants are kept growing with the minimum of moisture, just enough to keep them alive and it is the same for cuttings as it is for older plants. Dryness will not harm geraniums but wet conditions will. The plants also enjoy a dry atmosphere and so do well in a house with central heating. They retain their leaves the whole year through and continue to bear their flowers though mostly these are insignificant.

Propagation

Propagation is from cuttings which can be rooted at any time where a house or garden room is centrally heated; otherwise the best time is from April until October. During this time, in an average temperature of 60°F (15°C) there is little fear of the cuttings damping off before they root. They will root in from 15–20 days. Several cuttings can be taken from each plant together. They should be sturdy and short-jointed and be about 3 inches (7.5 centimetres) long. They should have the lower leaves removed so that these do not come in contact with the compost when planted, nor should the cuttings be asked to support more foliage than necessary whilst forming their roots. If rooting during the winter months, it is sound advice to dip the ends in hormone powder which will encourage more rapid rooting, though during the warmer months this is not so necessary. When using hormone powder, make the base of the cutting moist with cotton wool so that the powder will adhere the better.

Geraniums love to be in contact with a rough surface when they will form their roots quickly and for this reason always root better when against the side of an earthenware pot but with the modern tendency to use lighter and cheaper plastic pots, it is necessary to use a gritty compost. This is made up of coarse sand or grit, and moist peat in equal amounts by bulk. Set the cuttings 2 inches (5 centimetres) apart with the ends inserted 1 inch (2.5 centimetres) deep. Make them firm and if the compost is moist, it is not necessary to water them in. Nor is it advisable to place plastic sheets over the pots for this may cause the cuttings to damp off. Keep the compost nicely moist and the room

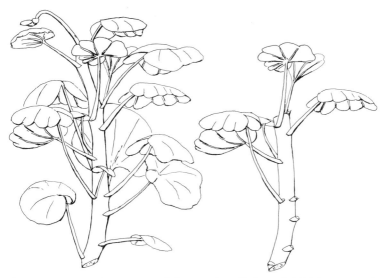

A geranium cutting removed for rooting (*left*) and (*right*) prepared for rooting

temperature at about 60°F (15°C). Do not use soil for the rooting unless it has been sterilized. If unsterilized soil is used, the cuttings may be troubled by Black Rot disease before they are rooted and will die back.

From stock plants growing in the home or garden room, it is possible to take several batches of cuttings each year. This will keep the plants tidy and will prevent them growing too big. To ensure rapid rooting, the best time to remove the cuttings is early April and again in September.

All that is necessary to maintain older plants in good condition is to provide a temperature of not less than 50°F (10°C) in winter and this is possible in almost every home. Between November and March, water sparingly giving a little around the side of the pots, perhaps once every two or three weeks and do not wet the foliage. In May, the plants can be moved to a sunny courtyard or to a terrace or verandah where, in the summer sunshine, the wood will ripen and the plants benefit from the gentle rains. The most compact are ideal plants for a windowbox. They are taken indoors again in October, before the frosts, though in the more favourable climatic parts of Britain, stock plants can stay outdoors all the year and will eventually grow into dense bushes as they do in their native Cape Province.

Growing on the Plants

Rooting will be confirmed by the cuttings taking on a paler green shade and if one is lifted, it will be found to have formed a dense bunch of roots at the base. It is now ready to re-pot and the compost should be an "open" one, from which surplus moisture can quickly drain. Geraniums like some decayed manure in their compost which may be cow manure or old mushroom-bed compost which will have lost any unpleasant smell. The plants also like a "sweet" compost, one containing some lime rubble (mortar) which can be obtained from old buildings; or use crushed chalk or limestone which is stocked by garden shops or builders' merchants. Do not use peat once they are rooted for it is too acid. The base of any compost should be a good turf loam but do not use old garden soil which is usually acid, due to the accumulation of soot and sulphur deposits over the years and which will also contain pests and disease spores. The compost should be made up of:

2 parts loam
1 part decayed manure
1 part grit

to which is added a small quantity of lime rubble, about a handful to a bucket of compost. Mix the ingredients well and do not forget to place crocks at the bottom of the pots for drainage before filling them.

A 3-inch (7.5-centimetre) pot will be large enough for the first planting and in three months, the plants will be ready to move to 6-inch (15-centimetre) pots in which they are sold after 2–3 months, or about 6 months from the time the cuttings were rooted.

When selling the plants, wrap each in clean white paper and as with all pot plants, insert a small plastic label with the name of the species or variety. This will be appreciated by the purchaser. There is no fear that the plants will come to any harm when moving them to the florist. There are no flowers of any note to drop their petals, whilst the leaves are rarely troubled by cold winds. Only dampness will harm them, especially in winter, so keep the compost on the dry side and do not water it until really necessary. A buoyant air temperature is also important.

Young plants can be grown in a window or in a light attic, possibly having one or more roof lights which can be opened in sunny weather. The plants do not want "coddling", they are amongst the hardiest of house plants and are intolerant of high temperatures and a humid atmosphere. During summer whenever the weather is dry, syringe the foliage when it will take on a new sparkle but do not do so if the weather is wet and humid, or in winter. The aim is to grow the plants as "hard" as possible when they will be short-jointed and grow bushy. They should be re-potted every 2–3 years, using the same compost but a slightly larger pot. When moving from one pot to another, do not disturb the roots. Leave the soil ball intact and merely add the fresh compost around it when in the new pot. Older plants will appreciate a handful of bonemeal added to the potting compost. Bone-meal is an organic fertilizer and releases its plant food slowly and this is what geraniums like best. Inorganic (artificial) fertilizers should not be used as they make for too much soft growth.

If kept dry, scented-leaf geraniums suffer neither from pests

Scented-leaf pelargonium, variety Mabel Gray. A grey-leaf variety of great beauty, the leaf veins being of dark green with leaves of maple-shape. They smell strongly of nutmeg when pressed

nor disease. They are one of the most foolproof of indoor plants and although not possessing the arresting beauty of the Rex begonias nor the intimate charm of the African violet, they have an interest and beauty all their own and are perhaps the easiest of all indoor plants to manage. Rarely on display in florists' shops, they usually sell on sight when they are.

Species and Varieties

Pelargonium asperum. The deeply cut leaves are of oak-leaf shape and appear as if covered with specks of gold. These are oil glands which release a resinous scent when pressed.

P. Attar of Roses. It makes a small neat plant with dainty leaves smelling of roses.

P. capitatum. The most common species of South Africa, it is a woody plant, its 3–5-lobed leaves being toothed at the margin and like the stems, are covered in short glandular hairs. When pressed, they release a powerful rose perfume. From this plant, attar of roses is made and sold in Algerian bazaars.

P. citriodorum. It has tiny leaves, like those of *P. crispum* and which release a refreshing lemon perfume when pressed. The small pale-mauve flowers have purple markings on the upper petals.

P. clorinda. One of the finest of the scented-leaf geraniums, its leaves smelling of eucalyptus with undertones of rose, whilst its orange flowers are borne in large trusses and are the equal of many show pelargoniums.

P. crispum. The variety *minor* makes a neat columnar plant, like a cypress tree, the small grey-green leaves, crisped at the edges, smelling strongly of lemon. The variety *variegatum* (in the USA, variegated *Prince Rupert*) is of similar habit but the leaves are attractively edged with cream.

P. filicifolium. From its name, the fern-like appearance of the leaves can be deducted. With its finely cut leaves it is more like a fern than a pelargonium and has a powerful resinous smell when handled.

P. fragrans. One of the most handsome species, making a plant of perfect shape, its neat silver-grey leaves smelling of pine woods.

P. Joy Lucille. A hybrid which has the deeply serrated leaves of one parent, *P. denticulatum*, and the peppermint scent of its other parent, *P. tomentosum*.

Ivy leaf pelargonium, L'Elegante. Not a scented-leaf variety but an excellent indoor plant of easy culture which enjoys conditions similar to the ivies

P. Lady Plymouth. A beautiful plant, the deeply serrated pale-green leaves being variegated with cream and releasing a pleasing rose perfume when pressed.

P. Moore's Victory. It has leaves like the oak which release the pungent smell of cayenne pepper when handled whilst its scarlet flowers are as large as those of *P. clorinda*.

P. odoratissimum. It is now a rare plant and has soft velvet-like leaves which smell of ripe apples. From the axils of the leaves it bears tiny white flowers held on long footstalks.

P. Prince of Orange. A hybrid of *P. citriodorum*, its small dark-green leaves smelling strongly of oranges.

P. Purple Unique. Its leaves have the smell of absinth whilst its large handsome flowers are of deepest purple.

P. quercifolium. The Oak-leaf geranium, its dark-green leaves, like those of the oak, releasing the warm pungent smell of incense. The variety Fair Helen makes a plant of more compact habit and has smaller leaves, whilst the flowers are of orchid-mauve.

P. radula rosea. One of the rose-scented geraniums, it was grown in Stuart times and with its neat habit is an ideal window-box plant. The leaves have narrow lobes and when pressed release a powerful rose perfume.

P. tomentosum. It has large, almost circular leaves held on long footstalks, both leaves and footstalks being densely covered in short hairs. All parts of the plant smell strongly of peppermint when handled.

6

Sink Gardens

The demand for sink and trough gardens—Preparing an old sink—Preparation of the compost—Dwarf trees for a sink garden—Plants for a sink garden—Small bulbs for a sink garden—Plants with grey or silver foliage—Flowering times of plants and bulbs for a sink garden

There are many townspeople who have to do their gardening in a confined space, possibly on a terrace or verandah or in a tiny basement courtyard so that it must take the form of containerized gardening whether it be growing plants in hanging baskets, pots or tubs each of which can be made most attractive. There is nothing lovelier than a sink garden, made from an old stone trough or an unwanted sink, possibly removed from an outhouse or the kitchen of a derelict building being pulled down to make way for new dwellings. Stone troughs are now rarely to be found and in any case are too heavy to move around but a sink removed from a terrace house will not usually be too deep and will measure only about 2 feet (60 centimetres) by 18 inches (45 centimetres) so that two people can easily move it even when it is filled with compost and plants. Or a sink garden can be made from cement and made even smaller, no more than 20 inches (50 centimetres) by 12 inches (20 centimetres), so that it can be handled by one person.

There is a constant demand for these sink gardens from all those who have only limited space in which to garden and there are those who live in the country and have possibly a paved garden which is admirable for sink gardens for they can be placed on stones along one side of a house or against a garden wall where the plants can be enjoyed from indoors and easily tended whatever the weather. They are delightful too for the aged and infirm since the sinks can be raised to any height above ground from 10 inches (25 centimetres) to 3 feet (90 centimetres) so that there will be the minimum of stooping when tending them. It is possible to look after a sink garden from a wheelchair.

A plumber of my acquaintance, whose wife is a keen gardener, has for years saved all the old porcelain sinks he has removed from dilapidated terraced houses and his wife makes them into the most charming sink gardens. These she advertises in the local newspaper and sells as many as she can make up, her husband delivering them in his van when working nearby. A small advertisement, no larger than a 2-inch (5-centimetre) single column, will not be too expensive and to catch the eye it is advisable to have a line drawing made of a sink filled with plants. This will enable the newspaper to have a block made for its reproduction and it can be used over and over again. A few words underneath suggesting that a sink garden makes an admirable present and will be colourful the whole year round, will usually bring many enquiries, some of which will result in definite orders for delivery on or near a certain date. The sinks can then be made up in plenty of time so that the plants will be established when presented.

There are many delightful plants that are at their best only in the gritty porous compost of a sink. They are the true alpine plants, those requiring scree conditions and there are few other places where they can be grown so well, except perhaps in pans in a cold greenhouse. They can also be grown and sold in small pots to those who wish to make up their own sink gardens.

A sink of suitable size can also be placed on a window sill provided it is made secure, where the plants will give hours of pleasure viewed from indoors. Or a small sink garden can be enjoyed inside a sunny window. But wherever they are grown the plants need sunlight and never do well in shade. They are natives of the exposed alpine regions and if a sink garden is to be placed in a courtyard, see that it is placed on the sunny side and away from tall trees from which rain can drip and fall on to the gardens, causing the soil to compact.

Preparing an Old Sink

To prepare a glazed sink (and alpine plants will not readily take to the slippery surface unless it is made rough) it must first be given a coating of cement on the inside. This will enable the plants' roots to get a grip, which they readily do when growing in a stone trough or a concrete sink. The coating is made by mixing together 1 part sand and 1 part cement with 2 parts peat which has first been made moist. Add only sufficient water when making up the mixture to bring the ingredients to a thick paste; it must not be made sloppy so that it will run off the sides when applied. It should adhere and be about half an inch (1.25 centimetres) thick. Do not make it too thick or it will take up more space than necessary. Before applying the mixture to a glazed surface, it will need treating with a bonding agent to make it stick as when fixing tiles on a concrete floor. Then put on the mixture as evenly as possible, leaving it quite rough and allow it a day or so to set hard.

The sinks should be treated under cover if possible so that the rains do not wash off the mixture before it has set. A small garden shed or a greenhouse is suitable to do the work in though the sinks can be left outside. Call and see your plumber and any others you know of locally and offer to make a payment of £2 or so for every sink they can deliver to you. In a small walled courtyard they can be stacked away tidily and will not be an eyesore either from the house or to neighbours. Several can be treated at one time and will be ready to fill when required.

The sinks will have a plug hole for drainage but should not be badly chipped on the outside as this will take from their appearance though any chipping on the inside is all to the good. It will enable the cement mixture to stick better. Do not bring the mixture over the edge of the sink as this will look unsightly when the sink is made up and is planted.

To make a trough or sink from cement, a mould will be required. This should be of seasoned timber and can be of any size but a sink of about 24 inches (60 centimetres) by 12 inches (30 centimetres) will not be too heavy to handle. The length could be nearer 20 inches (50 centimetres) and the width 10 inches (25 centimetres) without detracting from its appearance. Make it a standard size and such that you are able to manage. It should be no more than 4 inches (10 centimetres) deep with the base 1½ inches (about 4 centimetres) thick and the sides slightly more than 1 inch (about 3 centimetres). It must not be made heavier than necessary but must be strong enough to withstand carrying after it is made up with compost and the plants are set out.

The inside mould consists of a four-sided bottomless ''box'' made of ¾-inch (2-centimetre) thick timber. To make the mould

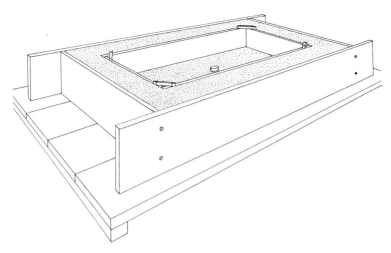

Preparing a concrete trough. The wooden moulds inside and out are made from hardwood

rigid, across the top at each corner fasten strips of thin wood secured by screws. The outer mould will be made slightly more than 1 inch (3 centimetres) larger all round and the best method is to screw together the sides so that when the cement has set, the screws can be removed when the four sides will fall outwards. Likewise, remove the screws holding the inner mould together at the top and gently prise the four pieces of wood inwards, the two end pieces first, removing these and then the larger pieces or sides.

On the inside of the outer mould mark a depth of about 1½ inches (4 centimetres) which will be for the thickness of the cement at the bottom.

The best method of making the trough is to place the outer mould on a piece of hardboard slightly larger than the mould, on a table or bench. Then mix up the cement. This should consist of 3 parts washed sand to 1 part cement and to each bucketful, mix in a handful of hydrated lime to improve the colour. The mixture should be of a consistency such that it can be poured. It must not be too dry nor too sloppy. Pour it into the larger mould to a depth of 1½ inches (say 4 centimetres) which has been marked on the inside and make sure the bench is level so that the base of the trough will be of the same depth overall. Now press in four large corks from wine bottles for drainage holes and allow the cement to dry completely but if it is thought best to provide the trough with additional strength, cut a piece of fine-mesh wire netting to cover the base and two longest sides not quite to the top and this is put in before the cement has set. Press the netting about half-way into the 1½-inch (4-centimetre) depth of cement, holding it in place with small panel pins on the inside of the mould. The pins will not pull against the netting when the sides are removed. The base of several troughs can be done at one time.

The next day when the cement is quite dry and has set hard, insert the inner mould and mix more cement of the same consistency, pouring it in between the sides of the two moulds. Allow it at least another 24 hours to set then remove the moulds, the inner one first. If wire netting has been used as a strengthener, this may show in places on the outside and more cement must be smeared on the outside of the trough, applying it with a trowel or smearing it over the sides with a piece of wood. Remove the corks and use them again.

If the moulds are made of strong seasoned timber, they will last for years and can be used over and over again. Nor will they warp with the moisture in the cement as unseasoned timber will do. Where possible, use hard wood and make the screw holes with a drill.

It will take a little practice to make up the cement to the right consistency and to have the troughs looking thoroughly professional, which is necessary before making them up. Brushing the outside of the trough with a hard bristle hand-brush will remove any rough bits of concrete and will leave the trough with a pleasant matt finish but do not do this or move the trough for another 24 hours, until the cement has set hard.

To enhance the dull grey appearance of a trough, paint it on the outside when almost dry with a solution of ferrous sulphate. This will give it the look of old Portland stone as it ages, it will become covered with lichens and moss and will have almost the look of real stone. The appearance may also be improved if a few lines are cut into the outside walls with a sharp knife whilst the cement is still not quite dry.

The next step is to immerse the inside of the trough in a solution of potassium permanganate and the best method is to replace the corks to seal up the drainage holes and to place the trough on the floor of a shed or greenhouse. Then make up a solution of potassium permanganate crystals which are dissolved in a bucket of cold water. Use 1 ounce or a handful for each trough and pour the solution into the trough, allowing it to remain for several days. This will neutralize any chemicals in the cement that might be harmful to the plants. Make up sufficient solution, which will be crimson-red in colour and is in no way harmful, to fill the trough completely. After several days, remove the corks and empty the trough of solution (perhaps into another) and wash it out with clean water. It is then ready to make up.

It may be possible to persuade the man about the home to prepare the troughs or sinks and for the housewife to do the making up which relies to a great extent on one's artistic ability in using plants. These may be grown in a frame placed in a courtyard or on a terrace, the plants in small pots.

Preparation of the Compost

The plants to be used in a trough or sink will need ample drainage which is provided by introducing plenty of grit into the compost for this is what the plants' roots need for healthy activity and to get a good hold. They will also grow into the cement sides which will be porous, like an earthenware pot, and will provide the plants with moisture and cool conditions during hot weather. For this reason it is important for the compost to contain some peat which will be retentive of moisture in summer. Do not use garden soil, even if it is available for the base as it will usually be full of weed seeds and this will spoil the appearance of the gardens when the seeds germinate. Obtain some turf loam or use the John Innes potting compost but if making up one's own compost use sterilized soil or soil from pasture land. See that it is a good fibrous loam and use 2 parts soil to 1 part each grit and peat or leaf mould. Mix well together and to each bucketful of compost add a handful of lime rubble (mortar) which will keep it sweet, also a sprinkling of superphosphate to stimulate root action. The compost should be nicely dampened and be in a friable condition when ready to use; not wet and sticky. Mix and store the compost under cover so that rain does not make it too wet and it does not become frosted.

A sink garden about 20 inches (50 centimetres) by 10 inches (25 centimetres) and 4 inches (10 centimetres) deep will need about 3 buckets of compost. Fill the sink to the top, pressing the compost well down at the sides so that there are no air pockets but first place some crocks or pieces of broken brick over the drainage holes. This will also prevent the soil falling through them. Use a table or bench to make up the sink. The work can be done in the kitchen as there is no unpleasant smell from the compost and if in a friable condition, it will hardly dirty the hands.

After filling the sink, cover the surface with shingle or spar chips. When planting, some of the small stones will percolate down to the roots to provide additional grit and drainage.

If it is desired to make up a sink to resemble an alpine meadow or a rocky outcrop, one or two pieces of limestone or porous tufa stone can be inserted into the soil. But do not push in the stone with the points sticking up above the surface of the compost. Instead several pieces should be set in layers, with the flattest part uppermost for this is how the stone is seen naturally, the stones having been worn away by wind and rain through the centuries. If two pieces of stone are used, perhaps in one corner of the sink, one should be inserted with the upper portion about 2 inches (5 centimetres) above the compost with the other near to it, but only about 1 inch (2.5 centimetres) of it should be showing above the compost to give a stepped or graduated effect. Pale-grey tufa stone, which is porous and so provides an entry for the plants' roots, will blend with the grey colour of a concrete trough but almost any kind of stone can be used provided it has a flat side. Set it well into the compost and to make it firm, press the compost tightly round it. A handful of spar chips around the base of the stone will provide a natural finish. A small tree can be set close to the stones and will add to the natural effect when it grows over them.

There are numerous alternatives to using stone in a sink and for those who are clever with their hands, a small rustic arch can be made and fixed just off centre of the garden, with a path of fine shingle leading up to and through the arch over which climbing miniature roses can be grown.

A delightful garden can be made by fixing into the base of a concrete trough, small panels of trellis or thin rustic posts with others fastened to the top horizontally. These can be glued together by using Bostik or another strong adhesive but the base of the uprights should be inserted into the base of the trough before the cement has set, or secure the trellis at the back with the compost. If the sides of the trough are to be 4 inches (10 centimetres) high, then have the uprights about 10 inches (25 centimetres) long.

As an alternative to fixing the posts around the sides, a row can be taken diagonally across the trough with pleasing effect if a miniature rose is planted against each post and trained over the top when the rest of the sink or trough should be confined to miniature roses rather than to alpine plants. A fairy rose garden will be as durable and as easy to manage as an alpine garden for the miniature roses are tiny replicas of the more vigorous floribundas and hybrid teas and are just as hardy.

Dwarf Trees for a Sink Garden

Abies balsamea. The balsam-scented fir tree and one of the best conifers for a sink for it grows as wide as it grows tall, rarely exceeding 6 inches (15 centimetres) in height. It is evergreen, the dark-green foliage being underlined with silver.

Acer palmatum atropurpureum. A miniature Japanese maple which produces gnarled stems and has small maple-shaped leaves of purple-bronze. Plant one near a stone in one corner of the sink and let it grow over it.

Cotoneaster, Stonefield Gnome. An evergreen with tiny glossy dark-green leaves and red berries. Slow growing, it takes on an ancient appearance when only 4 inches (10 centimetres) tall and is very long living.

Chamaecyparis. The cupressus or dwarf conifers are ideal plants for a sink garden for several are slow growing. They are evergreen too and provide a natural effect when planted against stones. Most are grafted on to a dwarfing rootstock and are imported from Holland. One of the best is *C. obtusa nana gracilis* which has gnarled stems and forms fan-shaped branches of dark-green leaves tipped with gold, whilst *aurea* makes a tiny tree of spreading habit and has golden-yellow foliage. *C. obtusa juniperoides* will have grown only 4 inches (10 centimetres) tall when it is ten years old and with its tiny leaves makes a beautifully rounded head of darkest green, whilst *tetragona aurea* forms a tiny almost stemless globe of golden moss-like foliage which virtually sits on the shingle. *C. pisifera nana* is also of upright habit with foliage of darkest green whilst the variety *squarrosus* has spreading fern-like branches of blue-green with a silver sheen.

Juniper. Many are suitable for a sink including *J. communis compressa* which forms a small upright plant of pencil slimness with dense feathery glaucous-green foliage whilst the variety *forrestii* has branches with pendulous tips.

Salix boydii. A weeping willow that will grow less than 10 inches (25 centimetres) high after 50 years. It has yellow stems and pale-green foliage which is particularly attractive when it unfolds in spring. It is an enchanting miniature tree to plant near a little bridge in the sink garden.

Spruce. The dwarf species are delightful plants for a trough and none more so than the Alberta White spruce, *Picea alba albertina*, which forms a pyramid of pale green and will grow less than 1 inch (2.5 centimetres) each year. Another charmer is *P. excelsa gregoryana* which will form a head of the size of a tennis ball with pale-green needle-like leaves. The variety *nana compacta* which is the dwarf Norway spruce, the Christmas tree, is equally slow growing and has horizontal branches. *P. abies procumbens* is even dwarfer, forming a dark-green hummock which hugs the ground.

The dwarf conifers and other trees are best grown in small pots so that they can be moved to the sink garden with the minimum of root disturbance. Young plants (or rooted cuttings) are obtainable from specialist growers for potting and are grown on in frames, the pots being placed closely together on a layer of shingle. Keep the plants moist at the roots in summer and give them a syringing with cold water each day whenever the weather is warm and dry. It may be advisable to keep the frames closed in midwinter so that the plants will not be damaged by hard frost which will spoil their appearance and from which they may take several years to recover. Give them very little water in winter, just sufficient to keep them alive.

One or more frames can be placed on the sunny side of a courtyard or on a terrace or verandah and the plants taken indoors when required, to make up into miniature gardens.

Set one or two dwarf trees, or shrublets, possibly in a group close to the stones and this will be the feature for grouping the other plants around them. These too may be grouped around a partly submerged stone or some other feature whilst dwarf bulbs may also be used to give colour in spring. These bulbs in many instances have attractive foliage which remains neat and tidy so that the bulbs take up the minimum of space. When the foliage dies down, it will be hidden by other plants and the bulbs will come up year after year.

Plants with colourful foliage should be used wherever possible for they provide interest in winter when the plants are not in bloom and a background for the small bulbs such as *Chionodoxa sardensis* which bears loose sprays of gentian-blue on 4-inch (10-centimetre) stems and is most attractive seen near the silvery-grey foliage of *Artemesia glacialis* or *Cerastium alpinum*.

Plants for a Sink Garden

Aethionema, Mavis Holmes. It is a tiny stiff glaucous-green shrublet growing 4 inches (10 centimetres) tall and during May and June bears large rose-pink flowers on short stems.

Androsace lanuginosa. One of the rock jasmines, it forms a woolly rosette and in May bears clusters of crimson flowers on 4-inch (10-centimetre) stems. *A. sarmentosa watkinsii* has woolly grey rosettes and bears bright-pink flowers, as does *A. sempervivoides* but here the foliage is dark green.

Artemisia glacialis. A tiny gem with silver-grey fern-like foliage.

Berberis corallina compacta. The smallest of the barberries, it is evergreen, with tiny glossy dark-green leaves and bears sprays of orange flowers in May.

Cerastium alpinum. This is not the trailing plant we know as Snow-in-Summer but is a tiny silvery-grey form growing only 2 inches (5 centimetres) tall and is a pleasing foil for dark-green plants. It bears sprays of white flowers all summer.

Dianthus. The little alpine pinks are most suitable for a sink, forming dainty tufts of narrow pointed silver-grey leaves and in June and July they bear double flowers of the size of a one-pence piece. One of the best is Elizabeth, the mauve-pink-flowers having an attractive brown centre. Another is Anne which bears cerise-pink flowers, whilst Bombardier has bright-red flowers which are most showy above the silver foliage.

Draba aizoides. A delightful little scree plant forming dark-green fluffy rosettes and bearing bright-yellow jasmine-like flowers in March and April on 2-inch (5-centimetre) stems.

Genista. The miniature brooms are delightful plants, bearing in May their tiny sweet-pea-like flowers. They make bushy little plants only 6 inches (15 centimetres) *G. januensis* bears tiny yellow flowers whilst *G. dalmatica* is a miniature gorse growing only 4 inches (10 centimetres) tall even when ten years old. It bears masses of yellow flowers on leafless stems.

Dianthus, Elizabeth

Geum montanum. Throughout summer it bears yellow almost stemless flowers which are followed by pretty fluffy seed pods.

Hedera minima. The smallest of the ivies which has neat dark-green leaves and makes a tiny shrublet 4 inches (10 centimetres) tall.

Iberis jordani. A little candytuft which makes a tuft of dark-green leaves and bears flat heads of snow-white flowers in June.

Jasminum parkeri. It has tiny leaves of darkest green and makes a small shrublet 6 inches (15 centimetres) tall, bearing its pale-yellow bells during summer.

Lychnis alpina. It bears pretty spikes of rosy-pink during April and May and is delightful when growing with the chionodoxas and scillas.

Micromeria corsica. A tiny aromatic shrublet growing 2 inches (5 centimetres) tall and bearing spikes of pinky-mauve during the latter weeks of summer.

Nierembergia rivularis. The Cup Flower whose white chalice-like

Left Two pipings as taken from a plant. *Right* The pipings prepared
for rooting

Pots of well-rooted pinks ready for planting out

blooms sit on 2-inch (5-centimetre) stems above a mat of dark-green leaves.

Pentstemon pinifolius. It is a tiny shrub with pine-like foliage and bears its scarlet trumpets from June until September.

Phlox subulata. They form sheets of brilliant colouring, Temiscaming being bright red; Auntie May, lavender-blue. Plant them at the edge of a sink and let them grow over the side.

Potentilla verna pygmaea. A plant of shrubby habit growing 2 inches (5 centimetres) high, it has dark-green foliage and bears golden blooms through summer. *P. tonguei* has silver foliage and bears flowers of rich apricot.

Primula clarkei. It is like a tiny auricula, making a rosette of bright-green leaves and on 2-inch (5-centimetre) stems bears its flowers of an exciting shade of deep rosy-carmine during March and April.

Raoulia australis. From the alpine regions of Central Europe, it has bright silver foliage which creeps along the ground and needs shingle to protect it from dampness. The tiny white flowers are insignificant.

Rose, miniature. The fairy roses which grow on 4–6 inches (10–15 centimetres) tall and make compact little bushes are perfect replicas of the large hybrid tea and floribunda roses and are ideal for sinks and troughs. They are usually planted by themselves for they do not associate well with alpine plants. Yet, perhaps surprisingly, the first, named *Rosa roulettii*, after Dr Roulet who discovered it, was found in the Swiss alpine village of Onnens. The plant grows 4 inches (10 centimetres) tall and the same in width and its little pink flowers are no larger than a one-pence piece. *Rosa peon* has double flowers of a deeper shade of pink and is just as compact, whilst Bo Peep has tiny flattish blooms of soft shell-pink. Two others that have retained their fairy-like quality are Elf, deepest crimson; and Pixie, a contrasting double white, like a tiny rambler rose.

The miniature roses are readily increased from cuttings taken when 2 inches (5 centimetres) long and inserted in pots of sand and peat. Move to small pots when rooted.

Saxifrage. For a trough or sink garden, those of the Kabschia or Cushion group are most suitable for their habit is compact and cushion-like with bright green foliage above which the flowers are borne on 2-inch (5-centimetre) or even shorter stems. *S. jenkinsae* has flowers of clearest pink whilst Hindhead Seedling is

Saxifrage burseriana crenata, a lovely sink garden plant

Saxifrages grown in a frame for planting in sink gardens

primrose yellow. Grace Farwell is especially attractive for it forms a silver-grey cushion and bears flowers of salmon-red. *S. aizoon baldensis* also forms tiny silver rosettes.

Sedum. The stonecrops are admirable plants for late-summer flowering and with their succulent leaves can survive many days without water. Most colourful is *S. cauticolum* from Japan which has glaucous foliage and rosy-red flowers. Another is Coral Carpet whose foliage turns deep coral-red whilst *S. spathulifolium*, Cappa Blanca from Oregon is the only stonecrop with silver-grey foliage and it bears golden flowers.

Soldanella alpina. Native of the Swiss Alps, it has dark-green almost circular leaves like those of the violet and on 3-inch (7.5-centimetre) stems bears its dancing circular flowers of mauve-pink with pretty fringed petals. It blooms in March and April.

Thymus serpyllum. One of the Mountain thymes, it spreads itself over the ground in a dense mat of darkest green, the variety *coccineus* bearing flowers of richest crimson whilst Bressingham is clear pink. The variety *minus* has the smallest leaves of any alpine plant.

Veronica cinerea. The small shrubby veronicas are ideal plants for a trough garden. This one has silver-grey foliage and early in summer bears spikes of brilliant blue on 3-inch (7.5-centimetre) stems. *V. pectinata rosea* is another beauty forming a dense grey mat, its spikes of pale pink held on 2-inch (5-centimetre) stems whilst the hybrid Trehane has golden leaves and sky-blue flowers.

Wahlenbergia serpylliflora. A plant of semi-shrubby habit, it forms a spreading mat above which it bears its purple bells on 2-inch (5-centimetre) stems. It is like a prostrate harebell.

All these plants are grown on in small pots in an open frame for they are completely hardy and are propagated in autumn or spring by division, or from cuttings as with dianthus, pentstemon and *Thymus serpyllum*. The shrubby plants which make woody stems are also best propagated by taking cuttings. These are removed when about 2 inches (5 centimetres) long using a pair of scissors to do so. They are inserted in pots containing a mixture of sand and peat (several to a pot) and kept moist. They root in about two months and are then grown on individually.

Plants propagated by division are removed from the pots and

gently "teased" apart, each piece having a small bunch of roots attached. They are replanted in small pots and grown on for six months when they are large enough to plant in a sink.

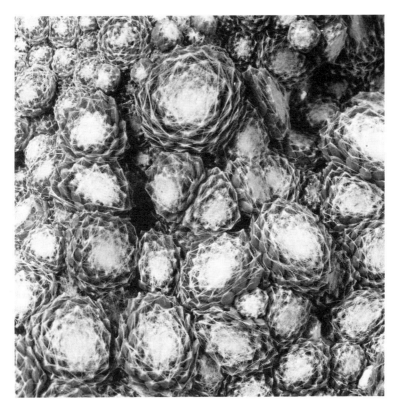

Sempervivums growing in small pots to use in sink gardens. These are Cob-webbed House Leeks

Small Bulbs for a Sink Garden

Once planted they last indefinitely and come into bloom year after year, increasing all the time. They will take up little space in a sink garden and should be planted in groups of three or four for best effect. They bloom in winter and spring before most other plants begin to flower and thus make it possible for a sink to be colourful almost the year through. This is a valuable selling point. In addition is the attractive foliage of several bulbs.

Chionodoxa. The species are amongst the most suitable bulbs for a sink garden on account of their neat foliage and their dainty flowers. *C. sardensis* blooms early in March, bearing its sprays of gentian-blue on 4-inch (10-centimetre) stems. At the month end blooms *C. luciliae*, its mid-blue flowers having a glistening white centre. There is also a pink form, *rosea*, and an all-white, *alba*. They are known as Glory of the Snow.

Crocus. Several species will bloom in autumn including *C. zonatus* which bears a small tapering bloom of rosy-lilac in September whilst *C. aitchisonii* bears a neat flower of china blue. In October comes *C. medius* with its flowers of deep purple opening like small chalices. In January, *C. fleischeri* appears above the shingle, its orange-red stigma visible through the white transparent petals. *C. korolkowi* follows in February, with its flowers of brilliant gold and in March comes *C. chrysanthus* and its many lovely varieties. The species are of more dainty habit than the Dutch hybrids which are more suitable for pots and garden planting.

Cyclamen. Several of the hardy species with their beautiful marbled heart-shaped leaves make suitable plants for a sink. Of compact habit is *C. cilicicium*, its dark-green leaves having a zone of silver whilst its small deep-pink flowers with their swept-back petals hover on 2-inch (5-centimetre) stems and it blooms in autumn. In bloom with it is *C. europaeum*, its foliage mottled with silver, its crimson flowers sweetly scented. *C. coum* is spring-flowering and has round dark-green leaves and bears crimson flowers. It has a white companion, *alba*.

Erythronium. The Dog's Tooth Violet, so called because the 1-inch (2.5-centimetre) long bulb is shaped like a dog's tooth and it has violet-purple flowers. The leaves are mottled with silver and bronze, above which the flowers hover like butterflies on 4-inch (10-centimetre) stems. Their delicate appearance belies their hardiness for neither snow nor cold winds will harm them when they appear in March.

Iris reticulata. With its netted bulbs this is one of the loveliest of the early spring bulbs. It has neat rush-like leaves and bears large purple flowers on 4-inch (10-centimetre) stems. They are

Erythronium dens-canis

deliciously scented and are like miniature Dutch irises. There is a lovely variety, Cantab, with sky-blue flowers. For maximum effect, plant two or three bulbs together, about 1 inch (2.5 centimetres) apart in autumn.

The smallest of all daffodils, *Narcissus minimus*

Narcissus. Several of the miniature daffodils are attractive in a sink garden, the best being the earliest and most dwarf of all, *N. minimus*, which bears its tiny golden trumpets on 3-inch (7.5-centimetre) stems in February. It is followed in March by *N. minor* which bears its yellow-lobed trumpets on a 4-inch

(10-centimetre) stem. With it blooms *N. cyclamineus*, so named because its golden reflexed trumpet is like a cyclamen flower. Later in the month, *N. bulbocodium* comes into bloom. It has rounded rush-like leaves and bears a golden flower shaped like an old-fashioned hoop petticoat with a wide circular rim, hence its country name. *N. canaliculatus* blooms at the same time. It has erect blue-green foliage and on each stem bears three or four tiny sweetly scented flowers resembling a polyanthus.

These lovely little daffodils may take a year or so to come into bloom but are well worth waiting for and once established they will increase each year.

Scilla. The most dainty of the spring-flowering squills are suitable for a sink garden. The first to bloom is *S. bifolia* which bears its twin-spikes of sky blue on 3-inch (7.5-centimetre) stems early in March. It is followed by *S. sibirica* from the bleak steppes of Siberia and which bears short spikes of blue or white, being quite unmindful of cold weather. Plant three or four bulbs together, almost touching.

Space can usually be found in a trough or sink for a few of the miniature bulbs to be planted in autumn after the "gardens" are made up. If bulbs have been used, inform the buyer so that they will not be disturbed when tending the "garden". Plant them about 2 inches (5 centimetres) deep with a trowel and after the "garden" has been planted cover the surface with shingle to retain moisture and to prevent heavy rain splashing soil on to the tiny plants and their flowers.

Plants with Grey or Silver Foliage

Artemisia glacialis
Cerastium alpinum
Dianthus, Elizabeth
Potentilla tonguei
Raoulia australis

Saxifrage aizoon baldensis
Saxifrage, Grace Farwell
Sedum spathulifolium
Veronica cinerea
Veronica pectinata

Flowering Times of Plants and Bulbs for a Sink Garden

Name	Flowering time	Colour
Aethionema, Mavis Holmes	May–June	Rose-pink
Androsace lanuginosa	May–June	Crimson
Androsace sarmentosa	May–June	Pink
Androsace sempervivoides	May–June	Pink

Name	Flowering time	Colour
Berberis corallina	May–June	Orange
Cerastium alpinum	June–August	White
Chionodoxa luciliae	April	Blue
Chionodoxa sardensis	March	Blue
Crocus aitchisonii	September	Sky blue
Crocus fleischeri	January	White
Crocus korolkowi	February	Yellow
Crocus medius	October	Purple
Crocus zonatus	September	Lilac-rose
Cyclamen cilicicium	September–October	Pink
Cyclamen coum	March–May	Crimson
Cyclamen europaeum	September–October	Crimson
Dianthus Anne	June–August	Cerise
Dianthus Elizabeth	June–August	Mauve-pink
Draba aizoides	March–April	Yellow
Erythronium dens-canis	March–April	Purple
Genista dalmatica	April–May	Yellow
Genista januensis	April–May	Yellow
Geum montanum	June–August	Yellow
Iberis jordani	June–July	White
Iris reticulata, Cantab	March–April	Sky blue
Jasminum parkeri	June–August	Yellow
Lynchnis alpina	April–May	Rose-pink
Micromeria corsica	July–August	Mauve
Narcissus buldobocium	April	Yellow
Narcissus canaliculatus	April	White
Narcissus cyclamineus	March	Yellow
Narcissus minimus	February	Yellow
Narcissus minor	March	Yellow
Nierembergia rivularis	July–August	White
Pentstemon pinifolius	June–September	Scarlet
Phlox subulata	June–September	Crimson
Potentilla tonguei	June–September	Apricot
Potentilla verna	June–September	Yellow
Primula clarkei	March–April	Carmine
Rosa peon	June–September	Pink
Saxifrage Grace Farwell	June–August	Salmon-red
Saxifrage Hindhead Seedling	June–August	Yellow
Saxifrage jenkinsae	June–August	Pink
Sedum cauticolum	August–September	Rose-red
Sedum spathulifolium	August–September	Yellow
Scilla bifolia	March	Blue
Scilla sibirica	March	Blue
Soldanella alpina	March–April	Mauve-pink
Thymus serpyllum Bressingham Hybrid	July–August	Pink
Thymus serpyllus coccineus	July–August	Crimson

Name	Flowering time	Colour
Veronica cinerea	June	Blue
Veronica pectinata	June	Pink
Veronica Trehane	June	Sky blue
Wahlenbergia serpyllifolia	June–August	Violet

7

Bonsai Gardens

Cultural requirements—Making the garden—Forms of bonsai—The art and maintenance of bonsai

With more and more people living in city flats, often in a basement which at one time may have been used only for storage, there has been a steady increase in the demand for indoor gardens in miniature, planted almost entirely with trees, thus bringing nature into the home, to be enjoyed by those who work in the towns, often in unpleasant surroundings. For centuries, the Japanese have been the masters of the art of dwarfing trees so that they can be grown indoors and they call it bonsai, which in Japanese means "plants in small containers". In Japanese homes the trees are used to make what are known as dish gardens, using pieces of limestone to provide a natural effect as seen in the landscape, with the gnarled and stunted trees growing amongst the rocks. City apartments and offices are filled with these little "gardens" which provide interest throughout the year. They are often placed in alcoves on plate-glass and are lighted by concealed fluorescent lamps which provide the trees with the light they require if they are to be long living. They must have light and are not happy in shade. They are living plants, the same as those found in their natural environment where they are exposed to wind and rain, frost and snow, fighting a continual battle against nature for their survival but they also receive plenty of sunlight, growing as they do in completely exposed positions. They are not trees of the woodlands but of rocky mountainous slopes where the soil is little more than a thin covering over the rocks. The trees can be grown indoors in a window but are best kept away from the direct rays of the midday sun which causes the compost to dry out too quickly. A window sill in a room facing north, east or west is ideal or they may be placed on a small table or stand some few feet away from a window. But if at the back of a room where there is only diffused light they will need fluorescent lighting to be successful.

Though where growing under natural conditions the trees survive extremes of temperature, they grow better where average temperatures prevail, such as those of a city flat or office warmed by central heating. A temperature of 60°–65°F (15°–18°C) by day and 55°–58°F (13°–14°C) by night will suit them well. They must not be placed too near a radiator or open fire as this will cause the trees to dry out too quickly. They require moisture and if the atmosphere is too dry, they should be given a syringing with lukewarm water each day. But they must never be given too much moisture at the roots. Maintain a buoyant atmosphere and keep the compost nicely moist but not wet. There should always be evaporation of moisture and if temperatures fall below 50°F (10°C) give no water until the compost has almost completely dried out. A too dry atmosphere or excess moisture at the roots may cause an outbreak of mildew which appears as small circular grey patches on the foliage of the plants and if not treated, the leaves will fall. Spray the plants with Murphy's Karathane but, above all, correct the conditions causing it.

A well-formed bonsai tree growing in its own pot

There is a considerable demand for bonsai gardens from people living in flats and from offices, banks and building societies for they create interest wherever they are seen and are in no way demanding in their care. Bonsai gardens are small. The containers used are shallow pans, either square or circular which take up little room and are easily moved from one place to another, being of no great weight.

Making the Garden

Glazed earthenware containers are the most suitable for bonsai gardens, or they may be made of cement and glazed on the outside. They should be of pale-grey appearance. If the containers are glazed on the inside the compost should contain a larger proportion of grit. There should also be drainage holes which are covered with crocks to prevent the holes being choked up and at the base should be a 1-inch (2.5-centimetre) layer of grit for additional drainage. Then add a layer of compost to a depth of about 4 inches (10 centimetres). The John Innes potting compost is suitable or if making one's own, use 2 parts fibrous turf loam to 1 part each peat and sand. Mix in a handful of mortar and a small handful (about 1 ounce) of bone-meal. A few pieces of crushed charcoal will keep the compost sweet. The compost should be in a friable condition, not too wet and use either turf loam from pasture-land or sterilized soil from a nurseryman. Do not use garden soil which will be full of weed seeds which will germinate in the warmth of a living-room and cause a great deal of trouble in removing them.

If stones are used to give a more natural effect, place one or more in the compost with the flat side uppermost. The stones should be not less than 4 inches (10 centimetres) in length and about 3 inches (7.5 centimetres) across and should make up about one-third of the surface of the container.

A completely natural effect can also be achieved by inserting two irregular stones about 2 inches (5 centimetres) apart and scraping away the soil between the stones to give the effect of a ravine. The compost removed is placed about the two outer sides of the stones and built up almost to cover the surfaces. Two trees can be planted on either side with one of very small proportions at the back of the ravine which should be covered with shingle, leaving the compost exposed at the outer edges of the stones.

The use of stones to create a natural effect is greatly to be preferred to using small ornaments.

After inserting the stones, press the compost around the edges and plant the trees in such a way as to obtain a natural effect. Never plant a tree in the centre of a pot or garden. Before planting, trim back any unduly long roots and spread out the fibrous roots carefully, packing the compost firmly around them. Water in the trees and stand the "gardens" in semi-shade for a week to allow the trees to settle in.

The trees can be bought from specialist growers in small pots and grown on in a frame on a terrace or in a courtyard until the "gardens" are made up. In winter, keep the frames closed but admit fresh air whenever the days are mild and sunny. In summer, remove the frame lights completely and in dry hot weather, syringe the plants daily. Bonsai gardens kept in the home or garden room should be put outdoors in summer if at all possible. Flat dwellers cannot do so but may be able to place the "gardens" on a terrace or verandah, where the plants will be invigorated by sunshine and gentle showers. They are taken indoors again in October when the trees will have taken on a fresh green appearance which they retain through winter.

Besides the numerous orders one may obtain for the "gardens", they may also be made up and given as presents on special occasions for they will be a permanent reminder of happy times, for bonsai "gardens" are more durable even than pot plants, a decade being only a short time in the life of the trees.

The "gardens" can be made up in the kitchen or in a well-lighted cellar and sold to florists or direct to one's private customers. All the materials needed will be the containers, some shingle and a few small pieces of limestone rock as well as the compost and, of course, the trees which are grown in their pots in a frame or on the sill of a window. The made-up "gardens" are not heavy and are in no way difficult to move about.

But before taking up bonsai gardening one will need to know something about the trees and their shapes and how to produce them for bonsai is a unique art, the Japanese for long being the masters and making full use of their knowledge handed down through the centuries, when constructing their rock gardens in the open in the same way that they make up their indoor gardens.

Forms of Bonsai

The trees must be naturally slow-growing with small neat leaves. Almost any tree in this category can be used in bonsai but the shaping of the trunk and its branches calls for patience and understanding. This is done by various methods which have their own classification. Dwarf conifers as used in sink gardens are not suitable for bonsai having lost the characteristics of the type.

Chokkan. This is the name for the upright tree often of pyramidal habit and amongst the most suitable are:

Chamaecyparis obtusa or Hinoki cypress.

Cryptomeria japonica: Japanese cedar.

Ginko biloba: Maidenhair tree.

Juniperus chinensis: Chinese juniper.

Pseudolarix amabilis: Golden larch.

The method is to select a tree about 18 inches (45 centimetres) tall and to cut back to about 3 inches (7.5 centimetres) of the main stem above the lowest branch. Thin wire is then coiled round the lowest branch, and the remaining portion of stem above it, so as to bring the branch into an upright position. Great care is needed in doing this. The branch then becomes the leader shoot and the tree is encouraged to form side shoots by removing the top inch (2.5 centimetres) of the new leader shoot, when the tree will take on a pyramid shape.

For a tree of umbrella shape, which is the reversal of the pyramid, the trees are raised from seed which is sown in spring and germinated in a small propagating unit in a temperature of 68°–70°F (20°C). Sow the seed thinly, using the John Innes sowing compost and only just cover the seed with sand. Keep the compost moist and transplant the seedlings to trays divided into compartments 1 inch (2.5 centimetres) square when large enough to handle. Grow on during the winter months in a closed frame and when 8 inches (20 centimetres) tall, transfer the seedlings with the roots intact, to 3-inch (7.5-centimetre) pots. Keep the stem straight by tying it to a small stick or cane and allow the first branch to form when about 6 inches (15 centimetres) above soil level, any lower branches being removed. During summer, pinch back the side shoots (branches) to two or three leaves and train the branches in an upwards direction by the use of wires. After two or three years, a small tree with a thick trunk and a spreading umbrella-shaped head will result.

In Chokkan it is the trunk that is of the greatest beauty and all branches to the front which hides the trunk are removed after planting the "garden".

Kyokkukan. This is a tree with a twisted trunk and for this, the Japanese Red Pine, *Pinus densiflora*, and the White Pine, *Pinus parviflora*, are the easiest to train but several of the flowering crab apples also respond to this method. *Pinus contorta*, the Beach pine, is also suitable.

With Kyokkukan, bonsai trees may be formed more quickly than by any other method and they are perhaps more symbolic of bonsai gardening than any other form. The trees should be 3–4 years old and should be potted. Around the base of the trunk wrap a small piece of canvas or sacking and wind copper wire around it. At a point equidistant from the base and the lowest branch, bend the tree without breaking it and wrap the wire round the branch. This is repeated with another branch in the opposite direction so that as it grows, the tree is much reduced in height. Using wire, the tips of the branchlets should be made to turn upwards to improve the outline.

Hankan. This method is used to form a tree with a gnarled trunk. Only the Japanese White pine is used and this is cleft grafted on to a seedling of the Red pine. The method was for long a closely guarded secret of the townspeople of Hanoi who have given their name to this form of bonsai. A graft is made on the stock plant about 6 inches (15 centimetres) above the base and it is this part of the plant that is twisted and coiled. Each coil is held in place by tying the coil with copper wire to a strong wooden peg driven into the soil. In Japan, this is done in the open where the plants remain for 12 months. The pegs are removed and the plants transferred to new ground. The roots are pruned back so that the plants will send out new fibrous roots and quickly re-establish itself. At this time, each branchlet on the upper portion of the stem is bent down as far as it will go and is held in place with other pegs. In 12 months, the leading shoot is removed and those branchlets more recently formed are fastened to the trunk by wires so that after four or five years, the trees will be only about 8 inches (20 centimetres) tall yet will have the appearance of wind-swept pines with the familiar gnarled trunk. This is one of the most popular forms of bonsai.

Shakan. This form is one of the easiest to obtain. It means a tree growing at an oblique angle, like a cordon apple, which restricts

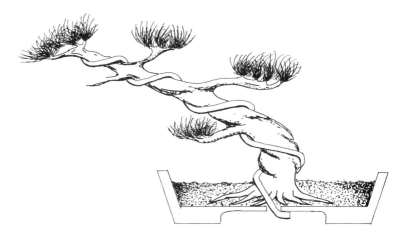

Kyokkukan, the form of bonsai by which trees are made to grow with a twisted trunk. Japanese red and white pines are the easiest to manage

Shakan, a bonsai from which, by the use of wires, a tree is made to grow at an oblique angle. The Japanese maples and willows respond well

the flow of sap and checks its growth. The Japanese pines respond well to this; also the willows, familiar on willow-pattern plates, and the lovely Japanese maples which are deciduous but whose new leaves each year take on glorious shades of purple, bronze and crimson as they unfold. *Acer palmatum atropurpureum* makes a beautifully spreading head and has crimson-purple foliage, whilst the variety Sangokaka has bright-red bark in winter and is handsome even when its leaves have fallen.

To grow at an oblique angle, the tree should have a low branch growing at right angles and about 4 inches (10 centimetres) above the base. Remove that part of the stem above the selected branch which is then fastened to a cane fixed well into the soil at the required oblique angle, 45 degrees, for maximum effect. When the branch has reached the required length, the tip is pinched back to encourage side shoots to form along the upper part of the stem and these in turn are continually pinched back.

Though the Japanese carry out most of the training of bonsai outdoors, it can be done indoors using bulb bowls and pots for the methods are exactly the same.

Kengai. For this method the Japanese maples and the flowering quince, *Cydonia japonica*, are suitable, the Japanese making use of almost all their native trees for bonsai. These trees make plenty of hard woody growth and are naturally slow-growing.

With Kengai, the tree is grown in cascade fashion. The method is to plant in a container at an angle of 45 degrees, with the soil ball just above the surrounding compost. Hold the tree in place with a cane as in Shakan. The main shoot is then brought over the side of the container as it forms and grows and is held down by wire fastened round the container. So that the wire will not cut through the bark, wrap a small piece of calico around the stem before fastening the wire to it.

So that the soil ball will not lift, plant firmly and continually press it down but to make absolutely sure, provide anchorage by inserting a small but strong wooden peg through the side of the soil ball and into the compost. This is done on the side opposite to that where the shoot or branch is being trained to cascade over the side.

Hankengai. Here the trees are trained almost horizontally and the method is somewhere between Kengai and Shakan, with the selected branch growing outwards, first at an angle of 45 degrees and gradually bringing it into a horizontal position by moving the cane to a more acute angle. The same plants are suitable to train in this way.

When a single tree is grown in a container this is known in bonsai as Ippon-ue and the tree of whatever style it represents is known as Tankan. Two trees in a pot or container is Sokan and here the effect is greater if one tree is taller than the other and both are of different shapes, one having a gnarled trunk; the other perhaps growing at an oblique angle. When two trees of different forms are used this is known as Yose-ue.

Acacias and robinias will form suckers in the container and these are retained. They will eventually give the appearance of several trees growing separately when in fact they are joined by underground stems. This is known as Te-tsuranari.

Another method is to obtain a tree with low horizontal branches which are spread out over the surface of the compost and pegged down. The leader shoot (that growing above the branches) is removed. From several points along the (pegged down) stems, where buds have formed, rooting will take place immediately below the buds and when the new shoots are several inches high, pinch them back to two buds to encourage them to grow bushy. The container will have the appearance of a woodland in miniature.

A similar effect can be obtained if a maple, cydonia or acacia has no horizontal branches. Any other branches are removed and the leader also. The tree is then planted along the surface of the compost with a proportion of its roots (the upward side) exposed and along the upper part of the trunk; the buds will "break" and grow upwards whilst roots will form on the lower side of the stem so that the container will be filled with individual trees. If required, these can be detached from the main trunk and lifted and replanted into other containers and the process repeated. This form of bonsai is known as Ikada-buki.

Yet another form of bonsai is Ishi-zuki. In this, the trees (and all are suitable to use) can be induced to grow with their roots clasped to a stone. This should be about the size of a tennis ball but with flat sides and it should have several fissures or openings as frequently occur in limestone or tufa, into which the roots are pressed.

Obtain some clay and bring it to a paste by mixing it with a little water. It should be of a consistency to enable it to be poured into the fissures which are above the level of the compost and into it several roots are pressed (using a toothpick or small piece of wood) whilst the other roots are inserted into the compost at the side of the stone when the tree is planted. Cover the roots with more clay and press into the fissures sphagnum moss if available or any type of moss obtained from old stones. Keep the clay moist when the roots will grow into the stone and each year will increase in size, giving the impression of very old trees growing in a rocky landscape with their roots exposed.

The Art and Maintenance of Bonsai

The aim must always be to imitate nature as closely as it is possible to do so, making the same use of stone as of the living trees. The methods of propagating and training the trees in bonsai is one of the most interesting forms of gardening but takes time to master. It is possible to attend local-authority run classes, with Japanese instructors, and classes are available at certain schools of floristry. To master the art takes several years and it may take a lifetime before one is thoroughly accomplished with the methods but once learnt, there is a lucrative career ahead in the making up and sale of bonsai gardens and giving lectures and classes of instruction. The work is light and can be done by a woman without the need for outside help in the preparation of the gardens whilst it gives one an interest all the year round.

Once the garden is made up, this does not mean that it will require no further attention. To maintain the trees in their dwarf form, they will need root pruning and this is done every three or four years. This may be done by scraping away some of the compost and with a sharp knife or scissors, cutting back any unduly long or thick roots before covering the roots again with fresh compost, packing it well around the roots. Root pruning will reduce leaf size as well as the size of the tree.

Top growth is restricted by pinching back the shoots at the end of each growing season. Deciduous trees need similar treatment, pinching back with finger and thumb all shoots to the third leaf. This will restrict the size of tree and enable it to form plenty of dense twiggy growth. Top growth is pruned early in autumn.

This is a suitable time to attend to the other plants, to remove decaying foliage and to give a light dressing of fresh compost. Remove any moss that has formed on the surface and afterwards give a covering of fresh shingle. A sprinkling of bone meal worked into the compost will provide valuable plant food.

Pests and diseases are usually present only when the trees have lost vigour due to their being over-watered or kept in the shade. A well-prepared compost, fresh air and careful watering will maintain the plants in a healthy condition. Mention has been made of mildew caused by a too damp atmosphere but greenfly may also be troublesome, causing stickiness and distortion of the foliage and greatly reducing the vigour of the plants by feeding on the sap. As a precaution, spray in spring and again in late summer with liquid derris before the plants are taken indoors for winter.

If you have to be away from home for any length of time, give the trees a long drink and wrap each (in its container) in a plastic bag when it will stay fresh for three weeks in a cool room.

Those who wish to grow their bonsai trees from seed can obtain packets of mixed seed to include Japanese Red and White pines, *Cydonia japonica*, juniper, Fuji cherries and other favourite Japanese trees, together with a complete sowing kit from Kent Country Nurseries of Challock, near Ashford, who also sell Japanese pines and other evergreens as young trees to train in the bonsai style for about £1 each. Trees already trained in one of the bonsai styles to use for making into bonsai gardens will cost about £4 each.

Thompson & Morgan of London Road, Ipswich, also sell packets of mixed conifer seed and deciduous trees as well as seeds of the popular bonsai trees separately. They also sell ceramic pans and dishes in suitable colours and with correct drainage holes. They cost about £3 each and are ready to make up into small bonsai gardens which sell for about £20 each depending on the type and age of trees grown.

8

Cacti and Other Succulents

Their requirements—Growing from seed—Transplanting the seedlings—Making a cactus garden—Propagation from cuttings—Troublesome pests—Cactus forms—Some other succulents

There is no more popular plant than the cactus, native of the desert lands of the New World where the plants receive very little moisture and almost perpetual sunshine. There is always a constant demand for these highly interesting plants, for schools or to have in the home, either grown in small pots or made into small cactus gardens. They are everyone's favourites for they are in no way demanding as to their culture; they are inexpensive and are very long-living. Given correct cultural treatment, there is no reason why they should not survive indefinitely as they do in their natural surroundings but although their requirements are simple, they are rarely given the basic conditions so necessary for their continued health and long life.

The chief cause of disappointment in growing cacti indoors is a yellowing of the plants, caused by lack of light. With but a few exceptions, they must have all the sunlight it is possible to give them which presents no problem when growing them indoors in the southern United States and in South America but in Britain and northern Europe, where in some years, there is a marked absence of sunlight, it is important to grow the plants in a window facing south or in a greenhouse or garden room. It is perfectly in order to bring the plants into shade for short periods, for a day or two if they are required for indoor decoration but this must be only occasionally. If kept in shade for any length of time, the plants become "drawn", losing their interesting characteristics and soon they turn yellow. If conditions are not quickly corrected, they will die.

In a house that I know, which was built early in the Victorian era and has large windows and wide sills, those rooms facing south are filled with small pots of cacti which stand in trays of damp shingle which supplies the plants with almost their total moisture requirements, not during the height of summer when they are watered at least once a week and maybe more often for the remainder of the year. Here the plants receive all the sunlight available, but even so they are turned each day so that those parts of the plants which may be shaded are in turn exposed to the full sunlight. Many hundreds of plants are grown in this way, raised from seed and propagated by offsets and are grown on until they are of saleable size when others take their place. The plants are sold in 2½-inch (6-centimetre) pots to chain stores and supermarkets as well as to local florists, in trays of ten or a dozen, each plant carrying a small plastic label with its name. Children find them of absorbing interest and are always on the look-out for new species and varieties to add to their collections. But they appeal to all ages for they are so labour-saving, not dropping their petals as do so many flowering plants whilst they do not need a high winter temperature to survive. The plants are quite happy indoors in a room (or greenhouse) temperature of not less than 46°F (8°C) in winter. At this, they will make little growth but will begin to grow again as soon as the sun gathers strength in spring. During winter, the plants require very little moisture for this is their rest period. They should not be completely dried off but only occasionally given a little water around the side of the pots. In winter, a dry atmosphere is essential or the plants will decay. This is why they do so well in a home with central heating, provided they are not in shade. In winter, in an unheated room and if the plants are close to the window, some protection from frost can be given by covering the plants with newspaper at night, also by day if the weather is severe.

During their rest period, the plants will take on a reddish tint which means that all is well with them. They will lose this when they receive more water in spring to aid the development of the flower buds, when the plants return to their rich green colour. If moisture is withheld at this time, the flower buds will fall and much of the beauty of the plants will be lost for it is during late spring and early summer that they bloom. At this time, the plants require more moisture than during the rest of the year for if the flowers are lost, so are the attractive berries that will follow. After flowering, the plants (or the cactus garden) can be placed out-doors, in full sun, when they will ripen during summer and autumn and are taken indoors again about mid-October. During summer they require plenty of fresh air and never at any time should be "coddled". On warm days open the windows.

Another reason for their popularity as house plants is that being succulents, they are able to store moisture in their foliage to use during dry periods, so that they can be left for several weeks in summer without attention if one has to be away from home and several months in winter in a temperature of around 50°F (10°C). Given just the little attention they need, they are almost foolproof and provide interest the whole year round.

Take care with their watering for if water is splashed on to the plants during summer when they are in direct sunlight, scorch-ing may result and in winter, areas of decay may set in if the water does not soon dry off. A golden rule with cacti is never to splash them when watering. It is better to apply the water around the side of the pot.

Those who do not have facilities in the home to grow cactus, and they will grow well in an attic with skylights and insulated against frost, will find they can make profitable use of a small greenhouse or garden room provided they are in full sunlight and it is possible to maintain a winter temperature of not less than 46°F (8°C). The plants can be grown on wooden shelves so as to make the full use of the structure and the most economic use of the heat employed. High temperatures are not required; gentle warmth only from early November until March, to maintain a dry atmosphere and to keep frost away. They also require plenty of fresh air.

Growing from Seed

Plants can be readily raised from seed. Specialist growers market the seeds as do the large seed-houses such as Thompson & Morgan of Ipswich. It is essential to obtain fresh seed for if more than a year old, it may not germinate. A temperature of 68°–70°F (about 20°C) is necessary for reliable germination and this is best provided by a small propagating unit installed in a greenhouse (where there is the electric supply available) or in the home, but it is also possible to germinate the seed outdoors in midsummer if sown in pans and covered with a sheet of glass or a plastic bag.

The seed can even be germinated in an airing cupboard which maintains a temperature of 68°–70°F (20°C) and in which the hot-water cylinder is fixed. If a warm cupboard is used, the compost in the seed pans must be kept moist and the pans inspected daily for as soon as the first seed has germinated, the pans are removed to a sunny window or to the greenhouse or garden room without delay. To get the seedlings used to the sunlight by degrees, the pans should however be placed in semi-shade for 48 hours before being placed in sunlight.

Before filling the seed pans or boxes with compost, place broken crocks or large pebbles over the drainage holes. A porous compost is desirable for seed sowing and this is necessary for the plants during their entire life. Soil is not necessary for seed germination though a little fine loam which has been sterilized can be included and helps to maintain moisture in the compost. A suitable compost is composed of 1 part fine loam (sterilized); 1 part silver sand; 1 part finely crushed lime rubble; and 1 part peat dust. Mix well together and use it almost dry. Fill the container, and an earthenware seed pan or bulb bowl is ideal, to about 1 inch (2 centimetres) of the rim (the reason for this will be obvious later) and lightly press it down after making sure the surface is quite level. If sterilized soil cannot be obtained, omit the soil altogether: do not use garden soil. Before sowing the seed, soak the compost.

Cactus seed is minute, almost dust-like and is sown more evenly if it is mixed with a little silver sand. Sow with finger and thumb, scattering it over the surface as evenly as possible. Do not cover the seed unless it be with a sprinkling of peat dust. The seed will work its way down amongst the grains of sand and peat particles. Do not water the seed before covering the pan with a piece of brown paper and a sheet of glass; or a plastic bag can be used. Plastic will keep the compost moist all the better for it must never be allowed to dry out or the seed will not germinate. On the other hand, it must not be kept in a saturated condition or the seeds will damp off. Keep a constant eye on the pans and give a daily syringing with lukewarm water (no more than mist-like) or whenever the surface of the compost appears dry.

In a temperature of 68°–70°F (20°C), the first seedlings will appear in 2–3 weeks if fresh seed has been sown, but it may take 5–6 months before all the seed has germinated. If a propagator is used, the seed can be sown in April but if sowing without artificial heat, it is better to delay the sowing until 1st June when there is more heat in the sun and the seed will continue to germinate throughout the summer months.

As soon as the first seedlings have appeared, remove the brown paper and if in a cupboard, remove the pans without delay. Do not disturb the first seedlings, wait until all (or almost all) have germinated after about 4–5 months, during which time they should be shaded from the heat of the midday sun otherwise they may be scorched. As soon as the brown paper is removed, whiten the inside of the glass. During this time keep a daily inspection for moisture requirements for the seedlings must never be allowed to dry out. As the first seedlings make growth it will be necessary to heighten the glass covering them or if indoors, to remove it as soon as the first seedlings to germinate have reached the glass. If a plastic bag is used, the same remarks apply. Sowing 1 inch (about 2 centimetres) below the rim of the box or pan will allow the first seedlings to germinate several weeks before they reach the glass or plastic covering, during which time the rest of the seeds may have germinated or at least most of them.

The seedlings of the various species differ greatly. The mammillarias and rebutias appear as tiny round beads which sit on the compost. They are without cotyledons. These are the first leaf-like growths characteristic of some cacti and most other plants. From the fleshy growths of the opuntias appear flat rounded pads covered with spines. If mixed seed has been sown, those seedlings forming cotyledons should be transplanted at the end of summer but those of bead-like formation are best left in the pans until the following spring. If the others are removed they will have more room to develop. Keep the compost slightly moist during winter and the seedlings growing in a temperature of not less than 48°F (9°C).

Transplanting the Seedlings

By early autumn the first seedlings will be ready to move into individual pots. These should be of 2½ inches (about 6 centimetres) diameter and preferably earthenware. They must not be glazed on the inside for cacti like to have their roots around the rough sides of a container, whilst they should always be grown in quite small pots. In this way their roots will soon reach the sides to which they will cling and will also use up any surplus moisture in the compost as quickly as possible. Cacti will turn yellow and will perhaps die back altogether if an excess of moisture has caused the compost to become stagnant. Vigorous root activity is of great importance so do not provide the plants with too large a pot. It is better to let them become almost pot-bound before moving them and then provide them with only a slightly larger pot. They must never lack lime in their diet and this is best given as mortar obtained from old walls which are being pulled down.

Crock each pot and then fill them almost to the rim. The potting compost should consist of 3 parts fibrous loam and 1 part each coarse sand or fine shingle; peat; and mortar or crushed lime-stone. Such a compost will not dry out too quickly yet will provide the plants with ample drainage and the grit which the roots so much enjoy. To each bucketful of compost, work in a handful of bone-meal. It is a more reliable source of plant food for cacti than decayed manure for bone-meal will have been sub-jected to high temperatures in its preparation and will be free of the troublesome Pithium baryanum disease which causes cacti seedlings to damp off. Also, as a further precaution against the disease, use Cheshunt Compound when watering, or Orthocide containing Captan. The compost should be in a friable condition when used and after filling the pots, allow 24 hours for the compost to consolidate before moving the seedlings.

Transplanting should be done with care for the seedlings form a single tap-root which will break off with the slightest pressure. Use a smooth-ended cane about 3 inches (7.5 centimetres) long to prise the seedling from the compost, taking care not to disturb others growing nearby and which it may not be advisable to move until spring. The smallest seedlings should be left to grow on during winter.

To transplant, hold the seedling between finger and thumb of one hand and transfer it to the newly filled pot, making a small hole with the cane for the root. After planting the root, gently cover with compost and press it firmly in. When transplanting is complete, water in with Cheshunt Compound, obtainable from most garden shops and stand the pots in a sunny window. During winter there should be little fear of the young plants being scorched by a too hot sun but if transplanting in spring and summer, it is advisable to shield the young plants from the direct rays of the sun by whitening the inside of the glass of a green-house or room. It is easily washed off later.

In winter, water with care, giving a little around the side of the pots whenever the compost appears dry. Overwatering in winter will cause the plants to damp off but they will rarely suffer if kept too dry. In winter, guard against draughts but in spring and summer, give the plants plenty of fresh air and as the sun increases in strength, increase too the waterings though guard against splashing the plants.

By springtime, the mammillarias and rebutias will be the size of marbles, and will have attained golf-ball size by the end of summer. They can then be sold in the pots or moved to slightly larger pots containing a similar compost but freshly made up and in this size pot they remain for several years before re-potting. Numerous offsets will form around the plants.

When re-potting, make sure the plants are at the same soil level as in their previous pots and this should be maintained throughout their life. Either leather or strong garden gloves should be used to handle the plants as they will be covered in spines; or wrap a wad of newspaper around the plants, holding it in place whilst turning over the pot to release the soil ball. Still holding the paper in place, transfer the plant with its soil ball intact to a larger pot and pack fresh compost around the side. Before moving the plant, water the compost so that it will not fall from the roots as it will if too dry.

Whether growing in pots or in a container used to make up a cactus garden, re-potting will be necessary only once in every three years.

Making a Cactus Garden

A miniature cactus garden can be made in a concrete or earthenware bulb bowl such as are used for tulips or hyacinths at Christmas. The bowl will be about 6 inches (15 centimetres) deep and 8 inches (20 centimetres) diameter and it is better if the inside is not glazed. The bowl must be well crocked at the bottom and then filled with compost to within 1 inch (2.5 centimetres) of the rim. The compost should be the same as that made up for potting the young plants and well supplied with grit to assist drainage. Make the surface uneven with high and low areas whilst a piece of tufa stone could be used for natural effect, perhaps one of 3 inches (7.5

centimetres) by 2 inches (5 centimetres) pressed well into the compost with about 2 inches (5 centimetres) showing above the compost. Around it plant several rebutias which will grow little more than golf-ball size in ten years; yet they bloom at an early age. *R. pseudodeminuta* will bear several large flat deep-yellow flowers at the same time and *R. miniscula* bears orange-scarlet flowers. The mammillarias are also globular and can be planted at the side of the bowl, with one of the taller species, for example *M. gracilis*, at the back of the stone. These plants also bloom when young, the flowers being arranged in a circle around the outside of the plant, like a halo. Some plants have coloured spines whilst the flowers are followed by coloured fruits (berries). Plant with them one or two lithops, the "living stones" of South Africa, which grow only 1 inch (2.5 centimetres) tall and are so camouflaged as to appear exactly like the stones amongst which they grow. After planting, cover the surface of the compost with shingle, to give the garden a natural finish. These gardens are not expensive to produce if you are able to raise the plants from seed.

Cacti may also be increased from offsets which begin to form around the plants when they are about two years old. They are readily removed when the plants are moved to larger pots. Wrap a wad of paper around the older plant when removing it from the pot and carefully detach the offsets with the free hand. These are planted into fresh compost in small pots and grown on.

Propagation from Cuttings

Cacti can also be propagated from cuttings. These may take the form of pads as with the opuntias whose stems are joined together by flat almost circular sections and one or more can be removed at the point where one section is joined to another. The opuntias have no spines on the areoles and are easily handled. Dust the cut parts with flowers of sulphur to guard against damping off and then lay the cuttings on trays in a warm, dry room. The best time to take cuttings is during the summer months. After a few days (it may take a week or so) the severed part will have dried and it is then ready to insert into a rooting compost. This should be made up of 2 parts silver sand and 1 part each peat and sterilized loam. Do not use unsterilized soil. Fill a 3-inch (7.5-centimetre) deep box or seed pan to about half, then insert the cuttings 1 inch (2.5 centimetres) apart and so that the cut portion is just covered with compost. Make the cutting firm and cover with a sheet of glass which has been whitened to provide shade. Cuttings or young shoots (as well as offsets) are to be found around the base of the mammillarias and these are removed with a sharp knife or razor blade. Rub flowers of sulphur on to the severed part of the cutting and also on to that part of the plant from which the cutting was removed. Allow the cutting a day or so to dry, then insert the base in the rooting compost. Water only when necessary and if needed, try to moisten the compost without splashing water on to the cuttings. During summer, the cuttings will usually root in about a month and they are then potted and grown on.

All the succulent plants growing in small pots will benefit if the compost is covered with some very sharp grit. This will prevent the compost splashing on to the plants and it will keep it free from algae which tends to form over a period of time.

Troublesome Pests

Well-grown succulents will rarely be troubled by pests and diseases but it is important to keep them free from dust for this will obscure the direct rays of the sun which is so necessary for the health of the plants. Those plants with a smooth surface can be dusted regularly with a camel-hair brush or with a bunch of feathers whilst those with spines can be blown with the mouth and in this way will be kept clear. During summer, spray the plants occasionally, using a mist-like spray and this will refresh and clear any dust accumulated during winter. The secret of success is to provide the plants with ample sunlight, a gritty compost, plenty of fresh air, except when the weather is cold, and care with their watering. The most troublesome pest is the mealy bug, a small white beetle-like insect about 2 millimetres long and covered in a woolly coat which protects it from wet sprays. The bugs congregate on the plants, hiding amongst the hairy threads which are a feature of some cacti and they also collect on the roots. Those above ground can be exterminated by keeping a close look-out for their presence and then removing them with a pair of tweezers. Their presence about the roots may be expected if a plant turns yellow for no apparent reason. Remove it from the pot and open up the soil ball. Remove any pests that are seen to dip the roots in methylated spirits before re-potting. Greenfly are of the same family and like mealy bugs, suck the sap from the plants reducing its vitality. If noticed, dust the plants with derris powder.

Cacti form ribs or tubercles known as areoles from which are produced woolly threads, like white hairs and also spines. These are of all sizes, colours and shapes and add to the interest of the plants. The spines are numerous and rayed and in their natural environment protect the plants from animals. They are to be found in all colours including crimson, purple, yellow and white and are of various lengths. Often there is one long central spine, possibly awl-shaped, which is surrounded by smaller star-like spines numbering up to thirty or more in certain species.

Cactus Forms

All cacti with the exception of Pereskia and Opuntia are grouped under the heading Cereus which has been divided into eight sub-sections or groups but not all are suitable for pot culture. For example, *Tribe 1. Pereskia.* Has long stems and leaves and has limited ornamental value. The opuntias, which are of Tribe II, are divided into two main groups, those having flat stems divided

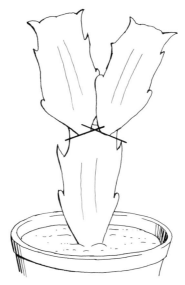

Cactus of the Opuntia type showing points of removal of the stems for rooting

into oblong or almost circular pads and those with cylindrical stems. Most grow into large trees in their native lands and are not suitable for pot culture. Of more than 300 species probably the best for pot culture is *Opuntia moelleri*, native of Mexico, and *O. clavata*. Both have oval stems which grow wide rather than tall and have long white spines though this is the exception with opuntias. The flowers are yellow and are followed by yellow fruits.

The *Ceraceae* (Tribe III) are suitable for pot culture. Mostly native of South America extending into the southern United States with the section Mammillaria almost entirely confined to Mexico. Many of this large tribe are ideal for small pots and cactus gardens. The stems are cylindrical, ribbed or columnar, the flowers funnel-shaped.

Cereus. Nocturnal flowering, the blooms being mostly white. The habit is upright, the rounded stems composed of four segments. They are bluish-green, *C. azureus* having a metallic-blue appearance and unlike most, it blooms when only a small plant. Most have pronounced spines but only a few species are suitable for pot culture including *C. jamacaru*.

Cephalocereus. Closely allied to Cereus, it produces masses of hair-like growths from the areoles, the genus comprises about 70 species including *C. senilis*, the "Old Man" cactus which produces from each areole about thirty strands of white hairs which may reach 6 inches (15 centimetres) in length and envelop the plant entirely. This is an interesting plant for pot culture and is readily raised from seed. Most of the species are night flowering. *C. phaeacanthus* is also lovely in pots. It has brown needle-like spines whilst its flowers are green on the outside.

Oreocereus. Mostly native of the Andes, the plants have rounded ribs and bear reddish-brown flowers. From the areoles at the top, long silky hairs are produced. *P. celsianus* is a most interesting plant and *O. trollii* is similar, with grey hairs and reddish spines.

Chamaecereus. There is only one species, *C. silvestrii*, which has short branched stems and bristle-like spines. It blooms profusely, its flowers being of an arresting scarlet-red colour.

Echinocereus. A genus of about 70 species, mostly native of the deserts of Wyoming and Texas and which are readily propagated from seed and cuttings. The plants are almost globular and are of easy culture, withstanding cold better than most whilst they bear their yellow or purple flowers at an early age. The spines are also coloured, those of *E. pectinatus* being pink, likewise the flowers. *E. enneacanthus* has an erect dark-green stem with 8–10 ribs whilst its flowers are brightest red. *E. glycimorphus* makes a spreading rounded plant with 6 or 7 ribs and from the areoles bears 8–10 awl-shaped spines and large reddish-purple flowers. *E. pulchellus* is equally free flowering, the grey-green plant forming 11 or 12 ribs and flowers which are pink inside, green on the outside.

Echinocactus. A small group which also has globular stems with prominent ribs and large areoles from which are produced numerous hairs and yellow flowers. *E. grusonii* is the Golden Ball which forms a spreading plant of tennis-ball size, its ribs having conical tubercles and golden spines. The yellow flowers are shaded brown on the outside.

Astrophytum. Known as the Star cacti on account of the star-like hairs which cover them, they were at one time included with Echinocactus and are of similar habit, the plants having the appearance of half an orange after it is peeled, forming 6–8 ribs or segments, along which the flowers are borne. They are yellow, with widely spreading petals. The species are amongst the easiest to grow and as they are shy to form offsets are best raised from seed. They are of easy culture, being tolerant of changes in temperature better than most. *A. myriostigma* is covered all over with grey star-like hairs so that the plant blends into the stony landscape. The yellow flowers are borne on the areoles at the top. *A. ornatum* is of cylindrical habit with yellow awl-shaped spines and flowers of clearest yellow.

Echinopsis. The plants are of similar shape to the astrophytums, though more flattened and broader at the top but with the same prominent ribs along which they bear large funnel-shaped flowers. No cacti are more free flowering, added to which is the rich perfume of several species, one being *E. leuchorhodantha* from the Argentine which forms about 20 ribs and has yellow spines whilst its pink and white flowers are richly scented. The dainty *E. polyancistra* with its slender white funnel-shaped flowers is also sweet-scented, likewise *E. multiplex* which forms 12–14 ribs with brown spines and pink flowers.

Lobivia. Their name is a corruption of Bolivia, their home and they are of similar habit to Echinopsis and the Star cacti, forming globular or ball-like plants with 12–14 ribs and bearing mostly carmine-pink or red flowers, those of *L. sublimiflora* measuring 2 inches (5 centimetres) across and with striking green stigmas. Several species which bear pale-yellow flowers are deliciously scented including *L. chrysantha*.

Rebutia. The plants more nearly resemble mammillarias in that they are not ribbed but produce tubercles (though less pronounced) which are arranged all round the stem whilst the small flowers, borne on the areoles, are of every colour imaginable excluding true blue. Their home is Argentina where they grow on mountainous slopes high above sea level so that under cultivation they are tolerant of changes in temperature. They are amongst the best cacti to grow in small pots for they do well in semi-shade and are most free flowering. The globular plants are depressed at the top and are pale green, *R. violaciflorea* being olive-green with 20 or more rows of tubercles each with as many spines whilst the deep-violet flowers are arranged in rows. *R. fiebrigii* is a plant of similar habit with the tubercles arranged in 18 spiral rows and bearing red flowers. *R. spegazziniana* is equally fine with its crimson-red flowers borne all round the base.

The rebutias form plenty of offsets which are readily detached and grown on in small pots.

Notocactus. Slow-growing globular plants with ribbed stems flowering at the top. The funnel-shaped flowers are about 3 inches (7.5 centimetres) long with reddish outer petals and yellow inner petals as in *N. concinnus* and they are freely produced. *N. scopalas* has a pale-green stem with 30 or more ribs whilst each areole produces 30–40 spines. The flowers are yellow. *N. ottonis* is also globular with 10–12 ribs, its flowers being reddish on the outside, yellow within.

Mammillaria. Probably the most interesting and important group, discovered in Mexico early in the nineteenth century and so named from the formation of the tubercles which resemble a nipple. The genus numbers more than 200 species, many with globular stems, and they make ideal pot plants. The plants form numerous offsets which grow into an attractive group if undisturbed. The plants require full sunlight and less moisture than other species. If care is not taken with their watering they will decay. Otherwise they are of easy culture.

One of the best for pots is *M. bocasana* which is a globular plant with cylindrical tubercles and from the areoles it produces fine silky hairs. The flowers are white tipped with red and are followed by red berries.

M. prolifera, native of Cuba and Haiti, is also globular with conical tubercles and from the areoles appear 5–9 radiating spines. The flowers are pale yellow followed by coral-red seeds. *M. schiedrana* is a dark-green globular plant with long white hairs and from the areoles appear 20–30 sharp radiating spines. The pretty flowers are white. *M. pseudonekei* has a cylindrical stem with white woolly hairs and as many as 30 stiff spines. The flowers are borne around the top and are red. *M. glochidiata* is globular and bright green, with cylindrical tubercles and bristle-like spines. The flowers are reddish-green on the outside, pink inside. *M. spinosissima* forms a cylindrical stem of bluish-green which is covered in wool and has thick erect spines. The beautiful flowers are borne around the top and are carmine-red, shaded brown on the outside. The mammillarias require plenty of lime rubble in their diet.

Few species of Tribes IV, V and VI are suitable for pot culture.

Tribe VII, the Epiphyllaneae, includes the epiphytic plants of the rain forests of the Amazon. They are shade-loving cacti, enjoying semi-shade in the home and are of easy culture. They are spineless with flat stems and the areoles are present along the edges. They require a porous soil and are propagated by rooting the stem sections, like the opuntias.

Of this group, *Zygocactus* is the familiar Christmas cactus of supermarkets and garden shops and the plants sell on sight from mid-October until January when they make an arresting display with the large pink or crimson flowers which are borne at the end of the flat stems. *Z. truncatus* is the best-known species and is of easy culture. The stems are divided into sections about ¾ inch (2 centimetres) wide and grow to almost any length, in their native South America, cascading from the stems of forest trees on which they grow, the flowers appearing from the end of each stem. Indoors in pots, they may be kept upright by the insertion of a few twigs amongst the stems but some are of more naturally upright habit.

As long as they are protected from frost they can be grown almost anywhere. Remove the stem sections at the point where each is joined to another and insert the end of the upright stem in boxes of sandy compost in a greenhouse or in the kitchen window. If kept moist, they will root in 3–4 weeks. Then pot singly into a porous compost enriched with some old mushroom bed compost and grow on in a greenhouse or garden room or even in the window of a room in the home so long as it is not in direct sunlight. This is a good cactus to grow in a shady room. The flowers have a long tube and protruding stamens and open to more than 1 inch (about 3 centimetres) wide. They remain in bloom for several weeks.

There are many lovely varieties, one of the best being *delicatus* which is of more erect habit with the flowers a combination of carmine and flesh pink. The flowers too, are of upright rather than pendent habit.

Some Other Succulents

Aloe. The aloe is of the lily family and is often mistaken for a cactus which it closely resembles. It is to the Old World what the cactus is to the New and is present in the desert lands and rocky outcrops of South and West Africa. Several species make excellent pot plants and require a similar compost and growing conditions to the cactus. Propagation is by seed and the offsets which appear around older plants. These can usually be detached with their roots from the parent plant and potted. The aloes are copious drinkers in summer but require only limited supplies of moisture in winter. Provide them with a minimum winter temperature of 45°F (7°C).

The best known is *A. variegata*, the Partridge-breasted aloe for its fleshy triangular leaves which terminate to a point are flecked with fawn in wide bands across the leaves at regular intervals from top to bottom. A well-grown plant in a 60-size pot is a fine sight. In spring it bears yellowish-red tubular glowers at the end of long stems held 10 inches (25 centimetres) above the foliage. Another attractive plant is *A. eru* which has long thin pointed leaves and bears yellow flowers in spring whilst *A. striata* has long grey leaves edged with pink which blend attractively with the coral-pink flowers.

Lithops. Like the aloes, they are native of the arid lands of South and West Africa and are known as living stones. They are small succulent plants with smooth sides and tops which are so beautifully camouflaged as to be almost indistinguishable from stones (pebbles) which litter the ground where they grow and where the plants survive for months without water. They are most interesting collectors' plants being of all sizes and shapes, some square, others round. They are ideal for small pots but are at their best in miniature gardens where they grow with stones of similar size and colourings.

Lithops are plants without leaves in the accepted sense and are of almost rubbery texture. In fact they have the feel of stones, being quite smooth. At the top of each plant is a slit, so thin as to be almost invisible to the eye in sunlight. Later, the slit widens to divide the plants into two halves which are really the leaves and from the opening, another tiny "stone" appears. The following year this will also divide and the original plant will, in time, form a rock-like clump of living stones. Towards the end of summer, at the centre will appear either a white or yellow flower, often being larger than the plant itself.

These interesting little plants are ideal for those living in a confined space. In the sunny window of a basement flat dozens can be grown in small pots. Later, some may be moved to larger pots in which they grow and multiply whilst some of the plants they produce can be re-potted and grown on separately. Use an earthenware pot if possible but a plastic pot will do if well crocked and a gritty compost is used. The compost should be made up of 2 parts silver sand and 1 part sterilized loam and mortar mixed together. Plant firmly but do not cover the body of the plant. Place them in full sun and do not over-water. Give them just enough moisture to keep them alive and do not worry if you have to be away from home for some time as they will survive several weeks without water.

Besides their flowers, the tops of the plants are covered with the most exquisite markings in crimson, fawn, brown, with some markings being in the form of squares. There are about a hundred species, each very different in appearance but all growing only 1 inch (2.5 centimetres) or so above the level of the compost. Their beauty will be enhanced if a little silver sand is sprinkled around the plants after potting. They are troubled neither by pests nor disease but over-watering is detrimental and try not to wet the plants themselves. Give a little water around the side of the pots, only perhaps once a month in winter. A minimum temperature of 45°F (7°C) should be maintained at this time.

Sedum. Several of this large family of succulent plants are suitable for pot culture. They belong to the same family as Sedum acre, the yellow stonecrop, native of the British Isles. They are of the genus Crassulaceae which includes the hardy semper-vivums. The sedums have their leaves arranged in pairs at right angles to the stems and they are thick and usually rough to the touch whilst they are of the most interesting colourings, some green, edged and shaded crimson; others yellowish-green edged with crimson and there are others which take on purple and bronze hues. The plants are of branching habit and in time form dense little bushes. A lovely one is *Sedum dasyphyllum* which grows only 1 inch (2.5 centimetres) tall and changes in colour through the seasons from silvery green to rose-pink and in June bears pretty pink and white flowers. *S. farinosum* is native of the Canary Isles and is also slow growing with deep-pink leaves shading to silver-grey. *S. lydium* is native of Asia Minor and grows 2 inches (5 centimetres) tall, its brilliant-green leaves turning to vivid red.

The sedums are readily propagated by cuttings which are treated like cacti whilst they require a similar compost, one which is well drained. Give them the minimum of moisture in winter but rather more in summer which they will store in their fleshy leaves and which will carry them through winter.

9

Miniature Roses

Where they can be grown—Their introduction—Their culture—Taking and rooting cuttings—Growing from seed—A fairy rose garden—Pests and diseases—Varieties

As gardening in confined spaces has become more of a necessity than a choice, so have the miniature roses, also known as Fairy Roses, gained in popularity. They are delightful plants, growing from 4 inches (10 centimetres) to 10 inches (25 centimetres) tall and just as bushy. They are completely hardy, known in America as sub-zero hybrids, and they can be grown in windowboxes and tubs and also in sink gardens. They are equally attractive when grown in small pots, the size depending upon the vigour of the variety. The pots may be placed on a window sill or on a terrace or verandah but wherever they are grown they must have sunlight. They are just as demanding in this respect as cacti and bonsai trees. They need the sun to ripen the wood without which they will not bloom freely. But such charm do they possess that they have become collector's items, many flat dwellers growing them in pots in the sunny window of a room facing south or west when they will bloom almost throughout the year and present few problems. They are tiny replicas of the large flowering hybrid tea and floribunda roses which need a garden in which to grow or at least a good-size tub. Not so the fairy roses which can be grown in 3-inch (7.5-centimetre) pots and can be used to make up the most charming miniature rose gardens to have in a basement court-yard or on a verandah which receives plenty of sunlight. That is all they ask for.

Since the Americans took up these little charmers after the Second World War, many new varieties have been introduced each year and this has greatly added to their popularity. Not all possess the dainty habit of some of the early introductions such

Miniature rose Red Imp growing in a 60-size pot

as Sweet Fairy and Bo Peep but in recent years the colour range has been widened so that whereas the flowers were mostly crimson, pink or white, they are now obtainable in the most exciting shades of orange, apricot and golden yellow though something of their daintiness of habit has been lost. Again, whereas the blooms were like tiny rambler roses, today many have the beauty of the hybrid tea rose and the freedom of flowering of the floribunda. They have also many uses other than growing them in a confined space. In a small town garden, they can be used as an edging to a path and they are even more attractive when planted in a double row, spacing the plants 12 inches (30 centimetres) apart. They may also be planted in small beds beneath a window and edged by a path of crazy paving. They are in no way out of place on a rock garden made of limestone which shows off the rich colours of the blooms to advantage. A rock garden comprised only of fairy roses with a few plants of the equally dainty violettas will be a charming sight in summer and if some of the miniature bulbs are planted in small groups beneath them, they will give colour in winter and spring. Such is the tremendous scope for sales of these little roses that one could earn handsome profits by growing them on a large scale to sell from home; also through the garden press as well as direct to florists, garden shops and supermarkets. The ladies find them irresistible when out shopping wherever they see them in bloom in small pots. They are long-flowering too, in a sunny window being in bloom from early June until the year end.

In a sunny window on a wide sill, as many as two dozen plants can be grown in 6-inch (15-centimetre) pots. This size of pot is needed to grow large stock plants which will give dozens of cuttings each year to root. A hundred years ago that great authority on rose growing, Shirley Hibberd, wrote: ''To propagate these roses is so easy, that an experienced hand will make a plant of every inch of wood that can be cut.'' This is so and from every two-year-old plant as many as two dozen cuttings can be rooted every year. From 25 plants this is 600 cuttings which will be ready to sell in 3-inch (7.5 centimetre) pots in twelve months' time at about 50p each wholesale. This will bring in some £250 and when once the stock plants have been bought, only some 3-inch (7.5-centimetre) plastic pots and compost for filling them will have to be purchased. Plastic pots of this size cost about £10 when obtained in 500s and 2 hundredweight of John Innes compost, required to fill them, will cost about £5 from a garden shop.

Additional plants can be grown in a sunny courtyard to use for cuttings. They are grown outdoors in large pots all year and are taken inside when the shoots are removed. They are then placed outside again to grow on for another year. The plants will have a long life if given a little attention. Re-pot them every two years

Miniature rose Frosty. It grows only 6 inches tall

using a mixture of turf loam or sterilized soil, coarse sand or grit and decayed manure in equal parts. After a year in the pots, and use 6-inch (15-centimetre) pots for stock plants, top dress with a little decayed manure or general fertilizer and re-pot after another 12 months. The pots must be well crocked so that winter moisture can drain away quickly. Stand them on flagstones or on a layer of shingle if placing them over an earth base. The plants are completely hardy and do not need to be grown in a frame but the use of a frame is necessary to grow on the cuttings both before and after rooting though they will root in a greenhouse, garden room or even an attic as long as it is sunny and well provided with skylights. Sixty cuttings can be rooted in a plastic or wooden seed box (5 rows of 12 cuttings), planting them about 1 inch (2.5 centimetres) apart so only 10 boxes are needed to root 600 cuttings. A kitchen table or a bench 6 feet (about 2 metres) long by 20 inches (50 centimetres) wide will hold this number.

Their Introduction

The fairy roses are not new; it is only now that gardening in a confined space has given them a new popularity and breeders have been quick to take advantage of it that they are becoming better known. Plants first reached Britain early in the nineteenth century, from Mauritius, to which island in the Indian Ocean they had been taken by travellers trading with China and Japan for these roses were rambler roses (*R. multiflora*) which had been dwarfed by oriental art probably many centuries before. In Britain it was called *R. chinensis* or the Dwarf Pink China rose and it grew about 6 inches (15 centimetres) tall. It was later called the Lawrence rose, *R. lawrenciana*, after Miss Molly Lawrence, a regular exhibitor at the Royal Academy, whose work on the rose species appeared in 1799. The Pink China rose created little interest in Britain or in France and by the end of the century it had disappeared from cultivation. Then in 1918, whilst on a visit to Omnens in the Swiss Alps, a plant was discovered by Dr Roulet growing in a pot on the window sill of a cottage, where it was said to have been growing for a hundred years and which the French doctor thought to be the long-lost dwarf China rose. He took the plant, after persuading the cottager to part with it, to Henri Correvon, a Swiss nurseryman who named it *R. roulettii*, after the finder though it was clearly a survivor of the dwarf Pink China rose, named in France Pompon de Paris.

It is a delightful plant, demanding attention in any company for it grows only 6 inches (15 centimetres) tall and bears tiny urn-shaped flowers of bright cerise-pink, so small as to fit inside a lady's wedding ring. What is more, the plant remains in bloom outdoors from 1st June until almost the year end if the weather is mild.

Yet once again its re-introduction caused little attention for this was an age of the opulent scarlet geranium and calceolaria, labour-intensive plants which were wintered in the luxury of a warm greenhouse where they were grown on a vast scale for summer bedding. The fairy rose was, however, taken up by a small nurseryman in Holland, John de Vink, who lived near Boskoop. He was one of the few people who could see a future for the little rose and he began crossing *R. roulettii* with the polyantha rose, Gloria Mundi, one of the first of the dwarf polyantha roses which were then becoming popular for bedding. The first crossing appeared in 1935 and it was a plant of true miniature proportions, like *R. roulettii*. It bore crimson flowers with a striking white centre, each flower opening to the size of a 5p piece. He named it *R. peon* and it is still much wanted by collectors. But this tiny seedling rose may never have appeared on the market had not Robert Pyle of the famous Pennsylvania rose firm, the Conard-Pyle Co., been on a visit to Boskoop in 1935 and heard about it. He was quick to realize its commercial possibilities and took out a patent for it in the USA, marketing it as Tom Thumb and it caused a sensation. From a share of the royalties, de Vink built himself a modern greenhouse and in 1938 raised the white variety, Pixie. Then came Midget and after the war, in 1946, appeared the deliciously scented Sweet Fairy which has Tom Thumb as one parent. Bo Peep followed in 1950 and Tinkerbell four years later. These roses became the toast of America, finding their way into New York apartments by way of department stores and florists. They quickly became collector's plants and the sunny windows of flats and houses everywhere were filled with the little plants growing in small pots. Enthusiasts with only a small back garden, and the room to erect a tiny greenhouse to raise seedlings, did so for the plant lends itself to hybridizing and many lovely new varieties have been raised in recent years by amateurs who have taken out patents and have become wealthy from the royalties. Yet no one in Britain has taken them up in the same way.

In an article in the *Gardener's Chronicle* in December 1922 Monsieur Correvon, who propagated the dwarf Pink China Rose and renamed it *R. roulettii*, said: ''It flowers perpetually and I have just gathered some little buds from under the snow that covers my garden.'' The fairy roses are indeed the ideal plants for the small modern garden, free and long-flowering and of compact habit and once planted (or grown in pots) they remain healthy for years. Their popularity is only just beginning and their culture could well be made a profitable small business for the housewife working at home.

Their Culture

To start with, obtain plants of no more than eight of the most dwarf varieties and possibly six plants who usually grow several varieties. The plants should be pot grown and will come with their soil ball intact and this is how miniature roses should always be grown as they do not like root disturbance. Again, by growing them in pots, they can be sold and planted at any time and they sell best when in bloom, from May until October when rose lovers cannot resist them. For stock plants, use 60-size pots (60 to a cast) or a 6-inch (15-centimetre) pot. If plants are obtained in spring, they are grown on for 12 months when they will be a dense mass of growth and it will be possible to take about a dozen cuttings from each plant. The stock plants are then top dressed and grown on outside in their pots which are placed in a sunny position and kept constantly supplied with moisture. Feeding them once a month with dilute manure water, obtained in concentrated form, of a proprietary made from a garden shop, will increase the plant's vigour and in 12 months' time the plants will again be full of cuttings to root.

Taking and Rooting Cuttings

The end of summer, August and September, is the right time to take and root the cuttings. By then the wood will be ripened by the sun but will not be too hard and so prove difficult to root, nor will it be too soft and damp off as might happen if the cuttings are removed too soon, in June or July. By mid-August, the wood will be in just the right condition and at this time of year the cuttings will root with the minimum of help. By October they will be ready to move to small pots in which the plants are sold the following summer.

When taking the cuttings, look over each plant carefully and remove them evenly from all round the plant, thus maintaining its balance. First, using scissors or a sharp knife, remove any unduly long shoots, selecting 8 to 9 from each plant. Remember to name each batch. Then trim each shoot to about 3 inches (7.5 centimetres) long, making the basal cut just below a leaf bud. Use only strong shoots from healthy plants, discarding all weak growth. Place the cuttings when prepared in rows on the bench and have ready the compost for filling the seed boxes (plastic or wood) in which they will root. The compost is made up of 2 parts sterilized loam and 1 part each coarse sand or grit and moist peat. If rooting only a few cuttings, they can be inserted in compost around the edge of an earthenware pot, about 10 to a 6-inch (15-centimetre) pot.

Before planting, to encourage them to root more quickly, for all hard-wood cuttings are more difficult to root, insert the base of the shoots in hormone powder. Seradix B is recommended. The method is to rub a pad of damp cotton wool over the base of each stem to moisten it and then to insert the end of the stem in the

Miniature rose cuttings prepared and ready for insertion

The cuttings are pressed firm

powder. In this way the powder will cling to it better. Then, using a dibber to make a hole in the compost which has filled the boxes to a depth of about 2 inches (5 centimetres), insert the base of the cutting about 1 inch (2.5 centimetres) deep and press the compost around it. The cuttings are set out a little over 1 inch (say 3 centimetres) apart so that 5 rows of 12 cuttings are inserted in a seed box. Preferably they should be all of one variety and clearly named.

If a cold frame is available to take the boxes (and 10–12 boxes can be placed in a frame 4 feet (say 120 centimetres) by 3 feet (90 centimetres), place them on a layer of shingle, close up the frame and shade the light with whitening, after watering in the cuttings which from now on must be kept nicely moist. If the days are sunny, give them a twice-daily syringing which will prevent them "flagging" and it will also help them to root more quickly. The cuttings will root just as easily in the sunny window of a kitchen or living-room but shield them from the midday sun by covering them with paper.

The cuttings can also be rooted in the garden by making a V-shaped trench 4 inches (10 centimetres) wide at the top and the same in depth. This will take a double row of cuttings inserted 2 inches (5 centimetres) apart into a specially prepared sandy compost. Make firm and in dry weather keep them moist. If the trench can be covered with tent-type cloches which, if of glass, have been whitened on the inside, or with transparent plastic, this will facilitate their rooting.

Under normal conditions, cuttings will root in 4–6 weeks which will be before the end of October, when they are carefully lifted from the compost and are replanted in small pots. Those rooting in the open will take a week or two longer.

Use 3-inch (7.5-centimetre) pots filled with a gritty compost made up of 2 parts loam obtained from pasture-land; and 1 part each grit and decayed manure, old mushroom bed compost being clean to use and most suitable. This will make for an open, well-drained compost but enriched with the necessary plant foods. If possible, stand the pots in the frame but now an additional frame of similar size will be needed. Close up the frame lights for a week or two until the plants are re-established, spraying them if the weather is warm but from early November until early March, they will require only the minimum of moisture, just enough to keep the plants growing, and water the compost rather than the plants. To prevent mildew, it will be advisable to dust the plants with sulphur and early in March, to persuade the plants to develop a bushy habit, remove the top 1 inch (2.5 centimetres) of stem. From this time, the plants will require more water.

On all mild sunny days in winter, give the plants plenty of fresh air. The fairy roses are completely hardy and must not be "coddled" in any way. From late March, remove the frame lights altogether, give the plants plenty of water and by early June they will have grown bushy, full of fresh young growth and flower buds. They can be sold in the pots as soon as the first flowers open.

Miniature roses as standards greatly increase the beauty of a sink garden when planted with the fairy roses by giving colour at a higher level. Or a standard can be used as a centre piece to a small bed.

To form a standard, do not pinch out the top of the main stem but instead, allow this to grow to the required height which may be about 16 inches (40 centimetres). Pinch out all side growths as they form for the first 12 inches (30 centimetres) of stem, then when the stem reaches 16 inches (40 centimetres), pinch out the growing point and allow the head to form. Do not remove the side shoots at the top but keep the lower 12 inches (30 centimetres) free of shoots. The plants will take about three years to form standards and as the stems grow quite thick, it will be necessary to provide them with plant food and a slightly larger pot. After 12 months, remove them to a 6-inch (15-centimetre) pot containing a compost made up of 2 parts turf loam and 1 part each shingle and mushroom bed compost. In this size of pot they will grow on for two more years when they are sold. Standards are sold for £2 or more for they take longer to develop and take up more space whilst the fairy roses from 3-inch (7.5-centimetre) pots sell for about £1 each retail or 50–60p wholesale which will leave a useful profit.

Growing From Seed

Miniature roses are readily grown from seed but if you wish to propagate the named varieties, this is done by taking cuttings. Growing from seed, however, is an inexpensive way of raising large numbers of plants and most will come true to type even if there are colour variations. Seedsmen sell the seeds as *R. polyantha nana multiflora* and a particularly reliable strain is Angel Rose, marketed by Hursts of Witham, Essex. One gram (about 250 seeds) costs £2 and many will produce fully double blooms of miniature rambler rose form in shades of red, crimson, pink and white so that a large proportion of the plants raised (possibly 20 dozen altogether) will be saleable. They are suitable for the cheaper markets catering for beginners, for connoisseurs prefer named varieties, some of which have urn-shaped blooms in the most exciting colours such as orange, salmon, pink and gold. But from plants grown from seed it may be possible to select one or two which are worthy of naming and propagating vegetatively. They must be of compact bushy habit, have considerable freedom of flowering whilst the flowers must be of a new colour in fairy roses, possibly cherry red or salmon-pink. When the plants begin to bloom, look for any unusual colours and grow on for a second year in a larger pot. If the plant still seems interesting, it may be worth naming and marketing as a new variety.

Seed is sown early in April, using the John Innes sowing compost. Sow thinly, using seed pans or boxes and as the seed is larger than that of most other flowering plants, it may be sown singly, spacing it out so as to allow each plant room to develop. Then lightly cover the seed with compost and water it in. If sown in April as the sun increases in strength each day, the seed container can be placed in a frame or on the sill of a sunny window. It will germinate more quickly in the dark so cover the pan with a sheet of glass and also with brown paper, removing both as soon as the first seeds have germinated. This will be in about a month but the compost must never be allowed to dry out. Remove the paper each day and syringe the surface when necessary. If sterilized soil was not used for the compost, it will be advisable to water with Cheshunt Compound as soon as the seed is sown so as to prevent the seedlings damping off.

Not all the seeds will germinate together: some may take up to 3 months but about 6 weeks after sowing, the first seedlings will be ready to transplant to small pots. At this stage use trays of Vacapots which are made of transparent plastic and divided into 1-inch (2.5-centimetre) squares. Fill them with the John Innes potting compost and plant firmly. After filling each tray with the seedlings, water in with Cheshunt Compound and place in a frame or window but shielding them from the direct rays of the sun for it will now be summertime. Keep the compost nicely moist but not wet. In another 2 or 3 weeks, more seedlings will be ready to transplant and at intervals throughout summer. Do not discard the seed boxes until the end of summer for the best plants may be the last to germinate.

By the end of summer, most of the seedlings will be ready to plant in 3-inch (7.5-centimetre) pots in which they will be sold the following year.

Firm planting is essential throughout the life of the plants if they are to retain their compact habit. Loose planting will cause them to form straggling shoots and the special character of the plants will be lost. When planting in the pots provide a compost made up of 2 parts loam and 1 part each grit and old mushroom compost. When moving to the pots, take care not to disturb the roots and do not plant too deeply. Just cover the roots and after planting, cover the compost with shingle. Water in and stand the pots in a frame where they remain all winter, admitting fresh air on all mild days. Do not give the plants too much water. They lose their leaves at this time and there is only limited root activity so they cannot use up large amounts of moisture until the sun becomes warmer in spring. Then step up the watering and pinch out the growing point and nip back any long shoots to encourage a bushy plant. In summer, syringe the plants often to prevent red spider being troublesome.

A Fairy Rose Garden

The fairy roses are at their loveliest when they are used to make up a sink or trough garden and this is another outlet for selling the plants. Being quite hardy, these gardens in miniature can be placed on a terrace or verandah or beneath the sitting-room window of a basement flat provided the plants can receive plenty of sunlight.

A sink garden can be made attractive by using some small flat stones to make a little path, possibly leading to a group of dwarf cupressus trees with the fairy roses grouped on either side of the path. Make the rose "garden" as natural as possible rather than planting in squares and use one or two of the creeping thymes for ground cover. When in bloom they blend admirably with the fairy roses. The dwarfs can also be used, planting in little groups of three or four. They will give winter colour and when the roses

A "sunken garden" of miniature roses. The garden wall is only
8 inches high

come into leaf in spring each year, they will hide the foliage of the
bulbs as it dies back.

Plant the roses about 4 inches (10 centimetres) apart and keep
the plants tidy and compact by removing any long shoots at the
end of each summer. Also, remove the dead blooms with scissors
and others will take their place in rapid succession. Water with
dilute manure water, which has no smell and is clean to use. This
will prolong and enhance the display by increasing the intensity
of colour of the flowers.

In autumn, give a light top dressing of peat and decayed
manure, working it right up to the plants; or in place of the
manure, scatter a little bone-meal over the surface and then give a
light dressing of sterilized loam and peat. Remove any weeds as
they are seen and keep the plants moist in dry weather by a daily
watering. The plants will also enjoy a syringing with cold water
each evening during hot weather and will respond with the
foliage taking on a rich green colour. The dwarf evergreens will
also benefit in the same way.

If there is space to make up one or two miniature gardens at
home, visitors who see them in bloom will often place orders for

one or more, possibly to give as presents to friends. A miniature rose garden need not be larger than 24 inches (60 centimetres) by 16 inches (40 centimetres) and made of cement. As the roses will be deeper rooting than alpine plants, make the "garden" about 5 inches (say 12 centimetres) deep so that after providing materials for efficient drainage, there will be a 4-inch (10-centimetre) depth of compost. This is made up of 2 parts sterilized soil or turf loam, and 1 part each shingle and old mushroom bed compost. The compost should be retentive of moisture in summer and well drained in winter. Miniature roses bloom for about eight months of the year in a sunny position and retain their leaves for about ten months. Only during the first 8–9 weeks of the year will the stems be bare and then the little bulbs will be in bloom.

Use only the most compact of the fairy roses for a sink garden or window box. These are:- *R. roulettii*, Bo Peep, Frosty, Tom Thumb, Mon Petit, Elf, Sweet Fairy and Cutie. These varieties have the almost perpetual flowering habit of the Pink China rose from which they are descended whilst they rarely exceed 5 inches (about 12 centimetres) in height. The blooms are of the size of an old silver 6d piece, no longer used in our currency, yet they may have dozens of tiny petals to give a bloom of perfect symmetry and which is enhanced by the striking golden stamens of some varieties.

Before starting a collection to propagate, it will be advisable to visit as many growers as possible, including the specialist rose and alpine plant growers so as to discover those which are the most dwarf and free flowering. Quite a few of the miniature roses, lovely as they are, will grow too tall for small pots and sink gardens. They are best planted in small beds in the garden or in tubs. They will grow from 8 inches (20 centimetres) to 12 inches (30 centimetres) tall and amongst these are Pour Toi, Rosina and Baby Gold Star, raised in Spain by Pedro Dot. They were the first miniatures to have yellow flowers, the blooms being of an exquisite urn-shape but the plants are rather too vigorous to be classed as fairy roses. Those raised in Holland by de Vink and given the names of nursery rhyme characters by the Americans for commercial reasons, are those of most compact habit.

A number of the fairy roses have "sported" or produced a climbing form in the same way that several hybrid teas have done, producing an extended shoot which may grow to 3 feet (1 metre) or more. Amongst the miniatures to have done so are

Pinkie, Orange Elf, Baby Jane and Fairy Princess. One may be planted in a sink garden and the shoots trained up thin rustic posts and along the posts fixed to the top as rambler roses do against rustic work in the garden. Set the posts well into the compost about 4 inches (10 centimetres) apart and so that there will be about 6 inches (15 centimetres) of post above compost level. The posts should be of the thickness of a 10p piece but less thick across the top. If the posts are fixed at the back of a sink garden, the effect will be charming, or they may be erected on either side of a tiny path, taken diagonally across the sink garden.

Pests and Diseases

Miniature roses are troubled by few pests and diseases, though when growing indoors, the plants may be troubled with grey mould. A bad attack will cause the flower buds to fall without opening, whilst the stems and leaves will be covered by a coating of grey "dust" which will release a cloud of white spores when the plants are moved. Where there is ample ventilation, rarely will the plants be troubled. Dusting the plants with Orthocide dust if the trouble is noticed will give control.

Mildew is also to be guarded against when growing indoors. It may appear on the foliage, stems and buds as grey spots which if not brought under control may spread and cover the whole plant in grey powder. Like all plant diseases, mildew will interfere with the proper functions of the plant, the leaves being unable to convert the carbohydrates into food with the result that the plant will lose vitality. The leaves too will fall prematurely. If observed, spray the plants with Karathane to the maker's instructions; or use it in the dust form. No preparations mentioned in this book are poisonous but even so, they should not be used in the kitchen where there is food about.

Of rose pests, greenfly may be most troublesome. They feed on the sap of the leaves and flower buds, causing malformation of the plant and its blooms and reducing its vitality. Spray with Dextrar, a non-poisonous derris extract or use it in the dust form. It will also eradicate thrips, small black flies which attack the plants in a similar way.

Red spider will be kept away if the plants are regularly sprayed in summer. They appear only under dry conditions. Should they be troublesome, dust with derris.

Varieties (Those growing no more than 6–8 inches, 15–20 centimetres tall).

Baby Crimson. Raised from *R. roulettii*, it grows about 7 inches (17.5 centimetres) tall and bushy. The blooms are of 5p-piece size and open flat. They are of deep rose-red.

Bo Peep. Introduced by Jan de Vink in 1950, it has retained its popularity. It makes a rounded bush 6 inches (15 centimetres) tall with pale-green leaves and bears fully double blooms of a lovely shade of candy pink. The tiny flowers have 36 petals.

Coralin. One of Pedro Dot's finest miniatures, it grows about 8 inches (20 centimetres) tall and its chalice-shaped blooms are of an unusual shade of coral-pink, shaded orange.

Cupid. A de Vink introduction, making a compact little bush 7 inches (17.5 centimetres) tall with brilliant green foliage and bearing elegant tapering buds of deepest pink.

Cutie. Growing 6 inches (15 centimetres) tall, it has the perpetual flowering habit of the China rose and bears tiny double blooms the size of a 5p piece, of a delicate shade of shell-pink.

Elf. Raised by de Vink it is the most dwarf of the miniature roses, growing only 4 inches (10 centimetres) tall, its tiny blooms are of the size of an old silver threepenny piece with 24 petals and of darkest crimson with prominent gold stamens. There is an orange "sport".

Fairyland. Introduced in the USA in 1960, it grows 7 inches (17.5 centimetres) tall and for weeks on end bears tiny blooms of rose-red. Each flower has 80 petals but for all that, they fit in a thimble.

Frosty. It was introduced in 1970 and grows 5 inches (10 centimetres) tall with glossy dark-green leaves and thornless stems, whilst its tiny white double flowers have the rich scent of honeysuckle.

Humpty Dumpty. Raised by de Vink in 1952, it has Tom Thumb as a parent and has since remained one of the most popular miniatures. It has glossy foliage and bears its flat carmine-pink flowers in large clusters. They are deliciously scented.

Little Flirt. It grows 7 inches (17.5 centimetres) tall with glossy foliage and bears tiny pointed buds of soft orange-pink shaded gold on the outside.

Maid Marion (Syn. *Red Imp*). Another of de Vink's Tom Thumb crosses, it rarely exceeds 6 inches (15 centimetres) in height and bears button-like blooms of dazzling crimson-red, like tiny multi-petalled rosettes.

Marilyn. Named in memory of Marilyn Munroe, it is a little charmer, growing 6 inches (15 centimetres) high and bearing throughout summer and autumn tiny double blooms of soft shell-pink.

Midget. One of de Vink's early introductions and a little pet, the pale-pink buds are only the size of a grain of wheat and open to bright crimson blooms less than a half-inch (about 1 centimetre) across with a striking white eye.

Mon Petit. One of the smallest, growing 4 inches (10 centimetres) tall and is almost perpetually in bloom. It has tiny fern-like leaves and bears small double blooms of a unique shade of cherry-red.

Mona Ruth. Though it grows less than 6 inches (15 centimetres) tall, it bears flowers almost 3 inches (7.5 centimetres) across which are purple and quartered like many of the old shrub roses.

Opal Jewel. It makes a compact little bush with small glossy leaves and bears hybrid tea-type blooms of soft satin-pink. The flowers have beautifully waved petals.

Pink Heather. It makes a tiny plant 6 inches (15 centimetres) high and bears masses of sweetly scented pompon-like flowers of a lovely shade of heather-pink.

Pixie. One of de Vink's introductions from his famous Ellen Poulsen—*R. peon* (Tom Thumb) cross, it has lace-like foliage and bears masses of urn-shaped blooms like tiny white "cabbage" roses which turn pink with age.

Robin. It grows 6 inches (15 centimetres) tall with glossy leaves of bottle-green whilst the tiny flowers of scarlet-red have attractively quilted petals and are borne in clusters.

R. roulettii. The original Pompon de Paris, re-discovered by Dr Roulet in Switzerland in 1918. It blooms in May and continues until almost the year end, each plant bearing hundreds of tiny urn-shaped blooms of rose-pink.

Simple Simon. It grows 6 inches (15 centimetres) tall with glossy foliage and bears tiny camellia-shaped blooms of a lovely shade of deep mauve-pink.

Sunbeam. The only real miniature of yellow colouring. It grows less than 8 inches (20 centimetres) tall with glossy foliage and bears tiny hybrid tea-shaped blooms of soft primrose yellow.

Sweet Fairy. A plant of perfect proportions, in 1960 it appeared

Miniature rose Pink Heather

in the "Top Twenty Roses" of the USA, the first miniature to do so. It makes a rounded little bush 6 inches (15 centimetres) tall with bottle-green foliage, and bears sweetly scented blooms of bright lilac-pink with elegantly pointed petals.

Sweet Vivid. Raised in the USA, it grows 6 inches (15 centimetres) tall and bears tiny salmon-pink flowers of perfect hybrid-tea form.

Tinkerbell. Another of de Vink's famous miniatures of Tom Thumb (*R. peon*) parentage, it grows 8 inches (20 centimetres) tall and bears chalice-like blooms of bright rose-pink, the blooms having as many as 65 petals although only little more than 1 inch (about 3 centimetres) wide when fully open.

Tom Thumb. (Syn. *R. peon*). The first seedling raised from *R. roulettii* and introduced by de Vink in 1935. When introduced by the Conard-Pyle Co. in the USA, it received an Award of Merit from the American Rose Society. It bears urn-shaped blooms of rich crimson and will come safely through sub-zero winter temperatures.

Tommy Tucker. It grows less than 6 inches (15 centimetres) tall and covers itself in trusses of button-shaped flowers of soft shell-pink.

10

Dwarf Chrysanthemums

Their value as pot plants—Their introduction—Rooting cuttings—Growing on the plants—Varieties

Whilst continuous supplies of chrysanthemums in pots are now available all the year round, grown by specialists in conditions of carefully controlled light and warmth so arranged that the plants will bloom out of season, it is in autumn and early winter that the demand is at its greatest and the home grower is able to cater for this trade by growing the hardy pompon varieties in 4–5 inch (10–12-centimetre) pots. Provided a sunny courtyard is available in which to stand out the plants in summer, they can be brought into bloom exactly at the right time but entirely without the use of heat or artificial light. Their culture is of the easiest and stock plants can be grown in the open in 4-inch- (10-centimetre-) deep boxes or, if in the cooler parts, in slightly deeper boxes so that the plants when cut back late in autumn, can be covered with a sheet of glass. This will provide extra warmth to bring on the cuttings and rooted offsets so that they will be of a suitable size for removing early in spring. A deep box covered with glass will take the place of a cold frame which can be used for other less hardy plants.

The culture of the dwarf early-flowering chrysanthemums is of the easiest. They were named pompons or pom-poms from their small double blooms resembling the pom-poms on the hats worn by French sailors for France was the place of their early popularity. The plants grow from 10 inches (25 centimetres) to 16 inches (40 centimetres) tall and are bushy, with the flowers borne in sprays. A well-grown plant will remain in bloom for 8 weeks or longer and there are early- and later-flowering varieties, to extend the season from mid-August until the end of November and later. There is always a demand for well-grown bushy plants, nicely presented with white paper enclosing the pot and lower part of the plant for even in difficult economic times, few shoppers can resist buying a plant in bloom and bud, so cheerful a sight do they present. They will cost about 80p so that the supplier to florists and supermarkets, can expect to receive about 50p for well-grown plants which must be bushy and compact for in this lies their charm. Those of most dwarf habit, which are usually the earliest to bloom, will require no staking but those slightly taller-growing are best supported by two small green sticks inserted into the compost on either side of the plant which is enclosed by a piece of green twine. The supports will scarcely be noticed.

To make a start, obtain a quantity of rooted cuttings in spring from one of the specialist growers such as Elmhouse Nurseries, of Walpole St Peter, Wisbech. They cost about £5 per 100 and if 250 are purchased in 5 varieties, this should give about 20 dozen saleable plants which, after the purchase of the plastic pots and compost should show a profit of £100 when sold in their pots.

Suttons Charm, a well-grown pot plant (*copyright Sutton & Sons Ltd*)

Uprooted cuttings are less expensive but a frame will be necessary for their rooting on a large scale and buying rooted cuttings will save much time and trouble to begin with anyway.

It will be possible to raise one's own plants by purchasing perhaps another 50 rooted cuttings (say 300 in all in perhaps 6 varieties) so that 50 plants can be retained. These are planted in deep boxes and grown on over winter, the offsets being detached in spring and planted in small pots. They are grown on exactly like rooted cuttings and are later moved to 4- or 5-inch (10–12-centimetre) pots in which they are sold. One root should give 5 or 6 offsets (which are small plants with roots attached to the parent plant) or some 300 from 50 roots, so that there will be about 20 dozen plants to grow on for sale and 50 or so to retain for stock purposes. There will have been no outlay in purchasing rooted cuttings on this occasion.

Their Introduction

The dwarf chrysanthemums are descended from the Chusan Daisy, introduced into Europe about the middle of the nineteenth century by Robert Fortune. In its native haunts this plant had to contend with extreme cold and so was quickly able to re-establish itself in the cold climate of Britain and northern Europe. By 1866 it had become so popular in the garden (where it grew 3–4 feet or about 1 metre tall) that Mrs Beeton writing in that year said: ''This little favourite has tended in no small degree to resuscitate the cultivation of the chrysanthemum'', which by then had lost much of its earlier popularity, due to the Victorians' love of more orderly gardening and the vogue for bedding out which lasted until the Second World War. Mrs Beeton would have been delighted to have been present when the yellow-flowering Denise appeared in 1950, the Victorians too, for it was the first of a new race of dwarf poms making a busy plant 12 inches (30 centimetres) tall and for the first time, chrysanthemums could be used for bedding. The blooms consisted of multitudes of quilled yellow petals packed tightly together and each flower was the size of a 5p piece. Other varieties followed in quick succession, mostly from the Elmhouse Nurseries, one of the finest being Allan Ruff, bearing chestnut-coloured flowers of the size of a 10p piece. Messrs Woolmans, the famous chrysanthemum growers of Solihull also took up the culture of these little plants and in the early 1960s were to introduce a series of varieties of even dwarfer habit. They called them Lilliputs, of which Redbreast, bearing button-like flowers of brightest red, is one of the best. All of them are ideal for small pots and with the new popularity of the small town house and high-rise flats, were in great demand and have remained so. The plants should be grown on a window sill or close to a window but sunlight is not necessary nor are high temperatures. Indeed, these chrysanthemums are amongst the hardiest and most trouble-free of all house plants and after flowering, can be stood out in their pots, cutting back the stems to 3 inches (7.5 centimetres) of soil level when in spring they will form offsets to grow on to flowering plants the following year. Or the plants can be set out in spring in a small border or in small beds when they will come into bloom early in autumn and remain colourful until almost the year end. Indoors, they require only a frost-free room and just sufficient water to keep them growing. As the blooms die, snip them off with scissors when others will take their place in long succession.

The plants are troubled by few pests and diseases. Mildew may attack the leaves in a cold wet spring and at this time it is advisable to dust the plants with flowers of sulphur which will prevent an attack and in summer, keep a close watch for leaf miner which if unchecked will spoil the plants intended for sale. The leaf miner is a tiny grey insect which lays its eggs on the underside of the leaves. Upon hatching, the larvae tunnel their way through the upper and lower layers of the leaves, leaving behind unsightly white lines. To deter the egg-laying females, spray the plants every fortnight from early June with a solution of 1 teaspoonful of Jeyes' Fluid dissolved in a gallon of water, taking care to reach all parts of the plants. An alternative is to spray with Lindex, at a strength of ¼ fluid ounce to a gallon of water. This will also kill aphis (greenfly) which may attack the ends of the shoots, sucking the sap, and if unchecked the plant will lose vitality and bear little bloom.

Rooting Cuttings

Dwarf chrysanthemums can be grown from cuttings in the window of a warm room or in a greenhouse heated in early spring to 48°–50°F (10°C). It is not necessary to begin rooting cuttings before mid-February, while those living south of the Thames can root their cuttings without using artificial heat for there will then be sufficient warmth in the sun to dry any moisture from the atmosphere in the greenhouse or frame. These chrysanthemums are completely hardy; cold will not harm them but excess moisture in the atmosphere will cause them to damp off. For those living in colder parts, a smokeless paraffin heater will keep the atmosphere buoyant and dusting the cuttings with flowers of sulphur will protect them from mildew. An example of their hardiness is recalled when, on one occasion during the very low temperatures and arctic conditions of a northern winter, several cuttings from a batch taken from some frame-grown roots which were removed late in January for rooting in a greenhouse, were dropped on the ground and were found only after a covering of ice and snow had melted several weeks later. When the cuttings were retrieved they were found to be in fresh condition and were rooted with no ill effects at all.

Cuttings can be purchased from specialist growers already prepared for inserting in boxes of compost or they can be removed from the year-old roots of plants which have previously flowered. The roots are packed closely together in fish boxes, then you press sterilized soil or compost around them. About 3 inches (7.5 centimetres) of stem is left on each root after cutting back the plants which is done towards the year end when they have finished flowering. Place the boxes in a closed frame or in a warm room or greenhouse and by mid-February numbers of cuttings or shoots about 2 inches (5 centimetres) tall will have appeared around the parent plants. These can be removed with a sharp knife, cutting them away about 1 inch (2.5 centimetres) below the level of the compost. The cuttings are then planted 1 inch (2.5 centimetres) apart into boxes of prepared rooting medium which may be composed of a mixture of sand and moist peat, both of which are virtually sterile and free of pests and disease spores; or use sterilized loam. Do not use ordinary garden soil which is not sterilized. Use a 2-inch (5-centimetre) depth of compost, make the surface level and insert the base of the cutting to a depth of about 1 inch (say 2 centimetres). Press it firmly in and if the compost is moist do not water, though it is advisable to dust the cuttings with sulphur. Do not let the compost dry out: keep it just moist and on sunny days, syringe the cuttings to prevent excessive transpiration of moisture. To prevent the cut-

Prepared cuttings ready for insertion in the rooting medium

Inserting the cuttings after they have been prepared

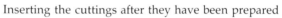

tings flagging on warm days it is advisable to shade them from the direct rays of the sun. Under favourable conditions, they will root in 3–4 weeks and as they do so will take on a fresh green appearance. They should then be moved without delay to small pots containing the John Innes potting compost and placed in a frame or a room window to grow on.

It will be even more labour saving to purchase, in early April, cuttings already rooted and to pot them up, standing them outside in a sheltered courtyard or in a frame; or one may propagate from the offsets or pull offs. These are cuttings with roots and appear from around those plants which have flowered the previous year. They may be growing in beds outdoors or the roots will have been packed close together in fish boxes as described. By about 1st April, the offsets will be about 3 inches (7.5 centimetres) tall and are detached from the old roots by gently tugging them away with pieces of root attached. They may then be planted into small pots in which they are grown for about 6 weeks when they are moved to 4- or 5-inch (10–12-centimetre) pots in which they are sold when in bud or bloom. They should be sold when the first flowers are opening so that the purchaser can enjoy the plant during the whole of its flowering period which will be from 8–10 weeks. For the amateur who has neither a frame nor warm greenhouse, propagation from offsets is a simple way of growing the plants. They will grow away as soon as planted and can be placed outdoors without any form of protection. Nothing could be easier. All that is necessary is to keep an eye on their watering, keeping the compost comfortably moist and syringing the plants during warm weather; and keep a sharp look-out for leaf miner and aphis.

Growing on the Plants

For their first potting, use a 3-inch (7.5-centimetre) plastic pot. Put a few chippings in the bottom for drainage and for the compost, use the John Innes potting compost or prepare one's own under cover to prevent it becoming too wet. A suitable compost is made up of 2 parts sterilized loam, obtainable from a nursery or garden shop; and 1 part each old mushroom bed compost and coarse sand. To each barrowful of compost, mix in 1 ounce of superphosphate to encourage vigorous root action and 1 ounce of sulphate of potash to build up a hardy plant. The compost should be in a friable condition and the ingredients mixed well together.

To pot, hold the rooted offset or cutting with one hand and with the other hand, work the compost about the roots, filling the pots almost to the top. Press the compost firmly, which is necessary if the plants are to grow compact and short-jointed, all-important qualities in dwarf chrysanthemums. After planting a batch of several dozen or more, water them in and stand outside in an open frame or sheltered position. Dust with flowers of sulphur and water when necessary which will be on most dry days. The plants will begin to grow away at once and within 4–5 weeks will be ready to move to larger pots.

For the final potting, which is done early in June, use a similar compost and a 5-inch (12.5-centimetre) pot. Knock the plant from the small pot by turning it upside down with the fingers of one hand held across the top of the compost and giving the pot a tap with a trowel held in the other hand. The plant will then come away with the soil ball intact and the roots will not be disturbed. Crock the larger pot, put a little fresh compost in the bottom to a

Examining the roots of a plant to see if it is ready for setting in a larger pot. Note the excellent root development

depth of about 2 inches (5 centimetres) and on this set the soil ball of the plant. Then work the fresh compost round the sides, making it firm, and bring the compost to just below the rim of the pot which will allow for watering. Give the plants a gentle watering and stand outside.

After a week in the larger pots, remove the growing point from each plant to encourage it to grow compact and bushy. Pinch out about 1 inch (2.5 centimetres) of the top of each plant and apart from watering and syringing the plants during dry weather and keeping a look-out for leaf miner, they will need no further attention unless it is thought necessary that the taller varieties require support as they reach maturity. Any unduly long shoots must be pinched back to maintain the shape of the plant.

The first varieties, those which bloom early, will begin to show colour towards the end of August. If they come on too quickly, stand them in a shady place for the main season for selling pot chrysanthemums does not begin until early September, when summer is over and people have returned from holidays. Of those varieties of dwarf compact habit which are most suitable for growing in pots, some colours will sell better than others and it may be that those flowering later will sell better than those flowering early. Experience in their culture will confirm which are the best-sellers.

A delightful way of using these dwarf chrysanthemums is to fasten strong wire around the rim of the pot and suspend them from an iron stake driven into the wall of a house or courtyard about 7–8 feet (2 metres) above ground. They can be watered by standing on steps or a stool. They may also be placed in a window box in their pots with sand or soil packed around the pots to prevent them being blown about by autumn winds. The plants should obtain all the moisture necessary from rain and dew.

Plants growing outside on a hard surface can be kept cool and moist at the roots by covering the pots with sand or soil which is kept moist in dry weather; or use a mixture of sand and peat. The pots can be wiped clean before the plants are sold.

The flowers of those varieties which bloom in November and December can be protected from adverse weather by standing the plants in a deep frame kept closed until they are sold; or place them in deep orange boxes obtainable from greengrocers and cover with plastic sheeting held in place with stones placed on the ground at the end of each row of boxes.

Varieties

Allan Ruff. It grows 10 inches (25 centimetres) tall and bushy and comes into bloom about 1st September, the flowers being almost 2 inches (10 centimetres) across and of a rich chestnut-bronze colour. It is one of the best for pot culture.

Billie Boy. Growing about 10 inches (25 centimetres) tall, it blooms early in September when it covers itself in masses of golden-yellow button-like flowers.

Blondie. It blooms from early September and grows a little over 12 inches (30 centimetres) tall and the same across. A well-grown plant will present a magnificent sight smothered in tiny double orange-bronze flowers.

Cameo. Growing about 15 inches (40 centimetres) tall but being of neat upright habit, it bears pure-white flowers which are solid with petals and are the size of golf balls.

Chick. It forms a compact round 12 inches (30 centimetres) high and almost as wide and by mid-September bears small double blooms of a unique shade of bronzy-pink.

Denise. The first of the dwarf pompons, it grows 12 inches (30 centimetres) tall and covers itself in bright yellow flowers tightly packed with tiny petals, to give them an almost globular appearance.

Fairy. One of the earliest to bloom, its primrose-yellow blooms opening before the end of August and it is one of the most free-flowering. It grows 10 inches (25 centimetres) tall.

Imp. Growing only 10 inches (25 centimetres) tall, it is truly an imp of a plant with its masses of rich red flowers and it blooms from mid-September until November.

Kim. It is at its best in October when a well-grown plant 16 inches (40 centimetres) tall is an arresting sight covered in double blooms of scarlet-bronze.

Lassie. It grows 16 inches (40 centimetres) tall and bushy, its button-like flowers of dusky pink appearing before the end of August.

Lilac Daisy. Growing 12 inches (30 centimetres) tall it bears its lilac-rose button-like blooms in long succession and they are seen at their loveliest under artificial light.

London's Pride. It grows 14 inches (35 centimetres) tall and blooms before the end of August, its button-like flowers of begonia-pink being of the size of a 5p piece.

Lustre. Of recent introduction, it makes a compact little plant and bears masses of tiny flowers of a unique shade of dull bronze, exactly the colour of lustre ware.

11

Bulb growing Indoors

Where to grow them—The rooting period—Bringing the
bulbs into bloom—Hardy bulbs for pot culture

Growing bulbs indoors in small pots is one of the easiest ways of
earning extra money at home and one of the most satisfying.
Artificial heat is not necessary but to bring the bulbs into bloom as
early as possible so as to take advantage of public demand for
out-of-season flowers, then some gentle warmth will be needed.
But there are many delightful bulbs which bloom during the latter
weeks of winter and early in spring which need little or no heat
and there are many that remain almost completely neglected by
those who cater for the pot-plant trade and indeed by those who
grow bulbs for pleasure in the home.

Amongst the easiest to grow and most beautiful of all bulbs is
Iris reticulata, so named because of its netted bulb tunic. It is a
perfect replica of a Spanish iris in miniature, growing only 5
inches (12.5 centimetres) tall and its flowers possess a delicious
scent. It blooms early in March when grown in pots indoors and
follows the snowdrop. When grown in pots, snowdrops sell on
sight if they are brought into bloom by the end of January and the
following month for they bring a touch of spring to the darkest
days of the year. In bloom at the same time is *Scilla sibirica*, a tiny
squill from the bleakest parts of Northern Asia which is like a
little bluebell and delights all who see it in bloom in small pots in
the late winter months. Shortly after comes the grape hyacinth,
its tiny globular flowers borne in short spikes on 5-inch (12.5-
centimetre) stems and it is also fragrant. Many of the tulip species
bloom early in spring, like the miniature daffodils which are
delightful in small pots.

Iris reticulata, Cantab

Where to Grow Them

Those who have a cellar, garage or shed will be able to make profitable use of each or all of them in growing the hardy bulbs. You will need a bench to do the potting and some bulb compost. Coconut fibre which is often sold for growing bulbs is not recommended as it provides little support for the bulbs and is difficult to keep moist. It can be used with sterilized loam and so can peat, using half and half, but neither peat nor fibre should be used on its own. Loam also gives better support to the growing bulbs.

To have the bulbs in bloom early in the year, they will need planting in October so make up the compost early in the month under cover for it should be in a nice friable condition when used. To every bucketful of compost, mix in a large handful of shingle to assist drainage or use some crushed oyster shell which is usually present in bulb fibres.

For all the small-flowered bulbs, small pots or bowls will be needed. These can be as small as 3-inch (7.5-centimetre) pots for scillas and snowdrops and as large as 5½ inches (about 14 centimetres) for hyacinths and tulips. The larger size should be "short" pots, known as "dwarfs" in the trade for they are not as deep as ordinary pots. They are ideal for all bulbs and are made of

Planting miniature iris bulbs

Multiflora hyacinths after planting

toughened polypropylene in a warm terracotta colour and have adequate drainage holes. They are light but strong and are easily stored one inside another. Pots by Sankey's or Ward's are obtainable from Hursts of Witham, Essex, who will quote trade prices if you are growing for sale. For 1981–2, Wards short 5½-inch bulb pots cost about £10 for 150 (about 7p each) and the ordinary 3-inch (7.5-centimetre) pots cost £12 for 500 (about 2½p each) so they are an inexpensive part of the cost of a pot of bulbs.

Order the pots and the bulbs at least a month before they are required for planting. Obtain the bulbs from a reliable firm such as Parkers of Chester Road, Old Trafford, Manchester, who will supply them at trade prices if you are growing for sale. They are a long-established firm and sell their bulbs at competitive prices.

To give some idea of prices, *Iris reticulata* bulbs cost £2.50 a 100 and about 8 will be needed for a short 5½-inch pot so that 100 bulbs will plant a dozen pots at a cost of about 20p each. The cost of the pot and its compost will cost another 10p and if no heat is used, 30p will be the total cost. Each pot will sell for about 50p either direct to callers or wholesale to florists and supermarkets, thus showing a useful profit. Snowdrops vary in price but single snowdrops cost about the same as dwarf irises. Four or five bulbs are planted in each 3-inch pot so that 20 pots will be available for sale from each 100 bulbs purchased. Total cost will be about 15p a pot and they sell for 25p wholesale and about 35p retail.

The secret of success in growing bulbs is to provide them with a suitable compost and to give them a long period in total darkness to enable them to form a vigorous root system. They will need at least 8 weeks in darkness, during which time they must be kept quite cool. Lack of success in growing bulbs indoors is due to one or more of several reasons such as too dry bulb fibre, too short a time being given to their rooting, and providing too warm a temperature whilst the bulbs are in the dark. It is a mistake to think you can hurry bulbs into bloom. If they do not form a satisfactory root system, the bulbs cannot make full use of the moisture in the compost and a stunted stem and flower will be the result. The same will happen if the compost is too dry or if the temperature is too high. Make an early start by planting the bulbs during the first days of October; use the right compost; and give them ample time to root. The rest is easy.

Have the compost on the bench and the pots close at hand. The small bulbs do not need deep planting, a little over 1 inch (say 3 centimetres) being the right depth for most of them, so if using a short pot, place in the bottom about 2 inches (5 centimetres) of compost. Then gently press in the bulbs, the broad or rooting end downwards. Space the bulbs evenly over the compost, about 2 inches (5 centimetres apart), then fill in with compost to about half an inch (about 2 centimetres) below the rim. Eight small bulbs will be planted in a short 5½-inch pot; about 4 tulips or daffodils; or 3 hyacinths which should be planted on only 1 inch (2.5-centimetres) of compost. When filling in, the entire bulb will then be covered but leave the neck exposed as for daffodils and hyacinths.

The Rooting Period

It will be necessary to select a cool dark place where the bulbs can root. A cellar is ideal. The pots can be placed in rows on the floor or on benches, thus making full use of the room. Or they can be placed at one end of a garage where there is room and if the garage has a window, either tack black polythene on the inside or cover the bulbs with a 2-inch (5-centimetre) layer of soil, sand or peat. A shed or outhouse will be equally useful. Give them no heat. The bulbs will be protected from excess rain and frost and that is all that is necessary. If the compost has been correctly prepared, they will need little or no water but the bulbs must not be kept in too dry a condition. If the weather is warm, spread damp newspaper over the pots to keep the compost moist.

If there is no place indoors for the bulbs to root, put them in a makeshift frame or plunge bed. This can be constructed from old railway sleepers laid on an asphalt or cement base (one sleeper placed on top of another will give the required depth) or from boards 6 inches (15 centimetres) wide where there is an earth base. The boards are held in place by wooden stakes driven into the ground and if a greater depth is needed for the pots, remove several inches of soil and put down a bed of shingle 1 inch (2.5 centimetres) deep on which to stand the pots. The pots can touch each other and if they can be covered with a frame light or with boards or black plastic sheeting, so much the better for this will protect them from too much moisture.

Light (especially sunlight) must be excluded during rooting, so tack black polythene on the frame light. If no protection at all can be given, place the pots in rows against a north wall or fence and

A plunge bed for pans of bulbs

cover them with a 4-inch (10-centimetre) depth of sand or soil to exclude light and frost. It will keep the bulbs cool without the compost becoming frozen.

A few pots of bulbs grown for one's own pleasure or to give to friends as presents can be placed under the kitchen sink; in an attic; or in a dark cupboard, but an airing cupboard will be too warm as will a centrally heated house if the temperature is too high. For at least 8 weeks after planting, the bulbs must be kept quite cool, in a temperature of no more than 48°F (9°C). Freezing will retard root action but will cause the bulbs no harm, though their rooting and flowering will be delayed.

During the rooting period, all that is necessary is to make sure the bulbs do not lack moisture, which so often happens when using bulb fibre on its own. Often the bulbs are planted in fibre or peat which has not been made sufficiently moist and it is difficult to add moisture at a later date. The result is that the foliage turns yellow and the flower is stunted.

Bringing the Bulbs into Bloom

At the end of November, uncover a pot, shake away the surplus soil or sand and with one hand across the top, turn the pot upside down and tap it to release the contents. If conditions have been right, it will be seen that the compost is filled with yellowish-white roots and is comfortably moist. It is now time to bring the bulbs into flower but with hardy bulbs, no attempt should be made to force them. Slowly introduce them to the warmth of a room or a greenhouse, at first heated to no more than 50°F (10°C) and in this temperature they are grown on for 2–3 weeks, giving them a little moisture whenever the compost begins to dry out. The bulbs will now have formed a vigorous rooting system and they can make use of any surplus moisture in the compost which they could not do before they formed roots. Too much moisture when they were dormant might cause the bulbs to decay.

The bulbs now require full light, though not necessarily sunlight and if there is no available space in the home or a greenhouse or garden room, keep them in a closed frame after shaking off the soil or sand used to cover them to exclude light. Do this carefully, one pot at a time, so as not to damage the shoots which may have grown into the soil covering. The shoots are brittle and easily broken. At first they will be pale yellow but gradually, after

2–3 weeks in the light, they will take on a deep-green colour. At no time should hardy bulbs be given high temperatures but snowdrops and scillas which can be placed in small batches in a temperature of 48°–50°F (9°–10°C) will come into bloom early in January when they sell like hot cakes to florists and super-markets. When one batch has been sold, another can be taken indoors and all the time those still in the frames will continue to grow and will bloom in early February in the warmth of the early spring sunshine without being given any artificial heat. They will be much in demand at this time but will not be quite so profitable as when they are brought into bloom in January.

By careful planning, it is possible to have bulbs to sell in pots from the first days of the new year until the end of March when daffodils and tulips from the Scilly Isles and the South West, grown without heat, begin to reach the market and the small grower cannot compete with them for price. Whilst the bulbs are rooting during the autumn, dwarf chrysanthemums in pots will bring in a useful income, then when the Christmas festivities are over, bulbs in pots will bring the first touch of springtime to shoppers during the dark dreary days of January.

As soon as the bulbs begin to bloom they should be sold, before the flowers are fully open, when the purchaser can enjoy them for several weeks. None of the small bulbs will need supporting but they are enhanced if the surface of the compost is covered with a little moist green sphagnum moss. Carefully press it around the base of the leaves and flower stems when the presentation will be much improved. Wipe the pots clean and wrap clean white paper around them enclosing the plants but leaving them open at the top.

If a heated greenhouse is not available, do not attempt to force hyacinths and tulips into bloom for the lucrative Christmas trade. To be successful, they require a minimum temperature of 62°F (17°C) and are better left to the specialists who grow them by the thousand in specially heated glasshouses. The hardy bulbs will open with the warmth of the spring sunshine if kept in a closed frame and for extra early bloom, a few pots can be placed on a window sill in a warm room.

Hardy Bulbs for Pot Culture

Chionodoxa. Native of the higher mountainous regions of Turkey and Asia Minor, they bloom in spring with the melting of the snow, hence their name from the Greek *chion*, snow, and *doxa*, glory. Louise Wilder, the famous American gardener described their flowers as being "like exquisite bits of enamel-work", which is an apt description. They are borne in dainty racemes on stems 4–6 inches (10–15 centimetres) long from the end of January until mid-March. Several species can be planted together in the short pots or pans, to give a long succession of bloom. The first to bloom is *C. sardensis* which bears sprays of 6–8 flowers on 4-inch (10-centimetre) stems. The flowers are of an intense gentian-blue colour. Then comes *C. luciliae* which has pear-shaped bulbs from which arise on 6-inch (15-centimetre) stems brilliant mid-blue flowers with a contrasting white centre. Later is *C. gigantea* with its larger flowers of clear mid-blue, like tiny lilies, and there is a white form, *alba*. Plant the bulbs about 1 inch (2.5 centimetres) apart in a 5½-inch pot.

Crocus. There are several delightful species that are attractive in pots although most of them do not remain as long in bloom as do scillas and snowdrops. It is, however, possible to enjoy a long succession of bloom by planting several species in a pot, say two or three corms of each. For indoor culture, plant a form of not less than 8-centimetre size, spacing them 1 inch (2.5 centimetres) apart and planting 2 inches (5 centimetres) deep. Plant the autumn- and early-winter-flowering species in July; the late-winter and spring-flowering species in September. They are delightful plants for a cold greenhouse but will bloom in a frame, when the pots can be taken indoors and placed on a window sill. Whilst rooting, keep the corms as dry as possible, giving just enough moisture to keep them growing.

Amongst the best species for pot culture is *Crocus imperati* named in honour of the Italian botanist Ferrante Imperato. It will bloom indoors at Christmas and during the first days of the New Year when its lilac-mauve flowers open to 4 inches (10 centimetres) across. They are heavily scented too. Also scented and in bloom at the same time is *C. laevigatus* which blooms longer than any other crocus, from early December indoors until March and is most valuable for pot culture. The flowers are white, feathered with purple on the outside. Another which remains long in bloom is *C. ancyrensis*, the orange flowers having blunt segments, feathered with bronze on the outside and they appear in January.

Crocus chrysanthus, native of the Balkans, blooms in early February indoors and makes a most generous display for each corm bears from 3–5 blooms. The type is golden-yellow but there are many named varieties, raised in Holland by Jan Hoog, one of the loveliest being Blue Peter, its clear blue flowers enhanced by a golden throat. E. A. Bowles has flowers of buttery yellow and Princess Beatrix is lobelia blue.

. The Dutch hybrids bloom a little later but make admirable pot plants with their large globular blooms. Paulus Potter is ruby-purple; Queen of the Blues, bluish-mauve; Kathleen Parlow, white; and Remembrance is purple.

Erythronium. This is the Dog's-tooth Violet, so named because the flower is violet-purple and the shining white bulb is shaped like a canine tooth. *E. dens-canis* is one of the loveliest of all bulbs for pot culture and it blooms early in February. Like the snowdrop, it must be grown quite cool and it likes a more peaty compost than most bulbs. Plant 5 or 6 bulbs to a short $5\frac{1}{2}$-inch pot, spacing them about 2 inches (5 centimetres) apart. Plant with the top of the bulb 1 inch (2.5 centimetres) below the level of the compost. The handsome lance-shaped leaves appear early in January and are dark green, marbled with cream and purple. Early in February appear the purple flowers which are borne solitary on 6-inch (15-centimetre) stems. They have swept-back petals which reveal 6 purple anthers. The variety Pink Perfection has clear pink flowers and Purple King has flowers of cyclamen-mauve edged with white. White Splendour has the largest flowers of all and they are as white as driven snow.

Galanthus. This is the snowdrop, which takes its botanic name from two Greek words, *gala*, milk, and *anthos*, a flower. In France it is *perce-neige*, appearing as it does through the melting snow. It is native of the woodlands of northern England and Scotland, extending across Europe as far east as the Caucasus. Johnson, who revised Gerard's *Herbal* in 1633, was the first to call it the snowdrop. The plant is intolerant of warm dry conditions and is rarely found in southern England and nowhere in the Scilly Isles. Indoors, the flowers open early in the new year and in small pots sell on sight for few can resist their charm during the bleak days of January.

Plant 4 or 5 bulbs in a 3-inch (7.5-centimetre) pot and use a 4-centimetre bulb. Anything smaller will not bloom the first year. Set the bulbs 2 inches (5 centimetres) deep.

An even better method is to lift several well-established clumps from the open ground in early November and to split them up into sections, each of which should fill a 3-inch (7.5-centimetre) pot. Place some fresh compost over them and keep the pots in a frame or in the open until 1st December when they can be moved indoors to bloom in a window. Or they can be left in a closed frame until they come into bloom in mid-January when they make the best price. Replant some of the divided clumps outside for they will grow into large plants in 2 years and can be divided again.

Galanthus nivalis is the common snowdrop of the British Isles and northern Europe and is the one grown in pots on a commercial scale. Other species are too expensive. It produces dark-green strap-like leaves 6 inches (15 centimetres) long and bears solitary drooping milk-white flowers on a 4-inch (10-centimetre) stem. Around the notch of the inner segments is an emerald-green crescent. There is a double form, *plenus*, whilst viride-spice has the outer segments tipped with green.

Hyacinth. A temperature of around 60°F (16°C) is required to bring prepared hyacinth bulbs into bloom for Christmas and, where this is possible, they are a profitable line. Either one bulb of

Snowdrops (*Galanthus nivalis*) in a cold frame in January

the large flowering hyacinths can be planted in a 3-inch (7.5-centimetre) pot or 3 bulbs in a short 5½-inch pot. For gentle forcing, use an 18-centimetre bulb for the large flowered varieties and a 14-centimetre bulb for the Roman hyacinths. These are the spray hyacinths, and what are known as multiflora hyacinths are derivatives. Each bulb will produce several loose spikes whereas the large-flowered *H. orientalis* hyacinths produce only one stiff stem of finger thickness and 10 inches (25 centimetres) tall, each with 50–60 bells arranged all around the stem and which open together and, as they do, release a powerful balsamic scent.

Specially prepared bulbs of those hyacinths which have been kept in cold storage are obtainable for planting early in September and they will bloom at Christmas. The bulbs should be kept in a dark, cool place for 8 weeks to form a heavy rooting system. Then early in November, place them in a temperature of 45°F (7°C), gradually increasing it until by the month end, it is about 60°F (15°C), during which time they will need copious amounts of water.

Fairy or multiflora hyacinths

Market them as soon as the first (lower) florets open and support the spikes by means of a wire, specially made for the purpose. One end has a loop to place round the stem, the other end is pressed into the compost.

Of many excellent varieties, Bismarck bears a thick spike of deepest blue; Jan Bos is ox-blood red; and Lady Derby, salmon pink. L'Innocence bears the largest spike of all and is pure white. Of the multifloras, Rosalie is shell-pink and Borah, blue. Ten top-size bulbs of prepared hyacinths cost about £1.50 so that 3 in a short 5½-inch pot will cost 45p and there is the cost of the pot and compost to add to this sum. They will sell for about 80p wholesale and £1.20 retail or say £1 if sold from home to those looking for something to give as a present or to enjoy oneself.

Iris. Of the large number of iris species, it is *Iris reticulata*, a dwarf bulbous form that is most suitable for pot culture. Native of the southern Caucasus and northern Iran, it is perfectly hardy and grows only 5 inches (12.5 centimetres) tall, its flowers measuring about 2 inches (5 centimetres) across when open, being tiny replicas of the Spanish irises, sold in large numbers in spring by florists.

The bulbs are enclosed in a net-like covering of fibre and are planted 5–6 to a short 5½-inch pot. They should be covered with 1 inch (2.5 centimetres) of compost. Make no attempt to force them. Place in a cool dark room or outdoors in a plunge bed or frame in February but if wanted earlier, they can be placed in a temperature of 45°F (7°C) in early January when they bloom at the month end. They are delicately scented. Cantab is one of the best, its flowers of Cambridge blue having an orange crest on the pale petals. Harmony bears flowers of pansy-purple and Royal Blue could have been better named Oxford Blue.

Iris histrioides is closely related and is grown in the same way. It grows only 4 inches (10 centimetres) tall, its flowers being of bright ultramarine blue, spotted with black. The form Major bears larger flowers than the type.

Muscari. This is the Grape Hyacinth and takes its botanic name from the Greek *moschos*, musk, a reference to the musk-like smell of *M. moschatum*, the Musk Hyacinth. There are several species suitable for pot culture, 4 or 5 bulbs being planted in a 4-inch (10-centimetre) pot and being completely hardy they are treated exactly like snowdrops. The species *M. armeniacum* makes a bulb up to 10 centimetres circumference and can be gently forced in a

Muscari botryoides album, Pearls of Spain

temperature of 45°F (7°C) when it will bloom in February. The flowers are cobalt-blue, borne in densely packed spikes and each tiny globular floret has a white rim. Blue Spike bears double flowers in an almost globular head and they are scented. *M. botryoides* grows 6 inches (15 centimetres) tall and has navy-blue flowers borne in a cylindrical spike and there is a white form, *album. M. conicum*, Heavenly Blue, is best known, bearing conical spikes of bright blue on 8-inch (20-centimetre) stems and it remains long in bloom.

Narcissus. All types are suitable for pot culture but as they bloom later in spring than most other bulbs, their profitability depends upon the amount of cut bloom available at this time. Though all are narcissi, the large trumpet narcissus is commonly known as a daffodil but those with small trumpets are usually called narcissi. Of all bulbs they need a longer rooting period, at least 12 weeks, and absolutely cool conditions if the blooms are to reach a degree of perfection which gives a pot or bowl of well-grown daffodils a beauty possessed by no other flowering plant. It is therefore necessary to plant the bulbs in early September, using what are known as first size double-nose bulbs. These will produce several flowers and if 4 or 5 are planted in a short 5½-inch pot, the display will be arresting.

Plant the bulbs firmly and with their noses (tops) just above the compost level. Place in the cellar or in a plunge bed until 1st December when they are taken indoors. They will then have made about 2 inches (5 centimetres) of top growth. At first, the room temperature should be about 45°F (7°C), gradually increasing it to 55°F (12°C) but no higher. As most daffodils reach a height of 14–16 inches (35–40 centimetres) they will need supporting. The blooms are heavy so when the buds begin to show colour (when they are sold) fix two or three thin green sticks around the pots and enclose the foliage and flower stems with green twine. When marketing, enclose the pots and the plants with white paper, leaving the top open. They will be in bloom about 1st February if they are grown in gentle heat but where no heat is available, they will take a month or 6 weeks longer and may miss the lucrative early market.

Of the large yellow trumpet varieties, Dutch Master is outstanding, the best ever raised, but Golden Harvest is excellent for pot culture and is early too. Of the white varieties, Beersheeba is of easy culture and of the large-cup narcissi, Carlton and Fortune are outstanding. Duke of Windsor has a broad white perianth (outer ring of petals) and a cup (corona) of apricot-orange, ruffled at the rim. Of the polyanthus or bunch-flowered narcissi, bearing 4–8 sweetly scented flowers to each stem, Geranium is striking with its pure-white perianth and short scarlet cup.

The cyclamen-flowered narcissi with their long trumpets and swept-back petals are most dainty, growing about 10 inches (25 centimetres) tall. Of these February Gold is a beauty and so is Peeping Tom. Of jonquils which bear 3–6 flowers to every stem,

Left   Narcissus tazetta,
Geranium

Below   Narcissus tazetta,
Laurens Koster

Narcissus triandrus albus, the Angel's Tears daffodil

Scilla sibirica, Spring Beauty

Trevithian has lemon-yellow flowers and forces well, likewise Laurens Koster which has white flowers with a yellow eye. Several of the miniature daffodils are ideally suited to pot culture, including N. *minimus* which blooms in January under glass entirely without heat. They grow less than 3 inches (7.5 centimetres) tall and bear bright-yellow flowers like Golden Harvest in miniature. Plant 3 bulbs to a 3-inch (7.5-centimetre) pot. They sell on sight. N. *minor* is only slightly larger and is a bi-colour, the perianth being pale yellow, the trumpet deep yellow. N. *triandrus*, which the cottager knows as Ganymeades Cup or Angel's Tears, is equally lovely, flowering in clusters of 3–9 on 6-inch (15-centimetre) stems. The perianth petals are swept back with the corona almost globular, like a tear drop. Plant 3 or 4 bulbs to a small pot and grow them like snowdrops.

Puschkinia. This hardy bulb, native of the mountainous slopes of Afghanistan and south Russia bears flowers of outstanding beauty and is ideal for pot culture. Plant 5 or 6 bulbs in a short 5½-inch pot and keep in a cool, dark place for 8 weeks. It will bloom in early March in a cold frame or greenhouse but in gentle warmth will flower in early February. It has strap-like leaves and bears its bell-shaped flowers in a raceme on a leafless stem 6 inches (15 centimetres) high. They are pale blue and open flat to reveal a bluish-green stripe down the centre of each petal quite unlike any other flower.

Scilla. The dwarf scillas, native of central Europe and Asia are amongst the hardiest bulbs and all are suitable for small pots. Plant 3 or 4 bulbs in a 3-inch (7.5-centimetre) pot; 5 or 6 in a short 5½-inch pot, setting them 2 inches (5 centimetres) deep. Keep them in a cool place for 2 months and place in a temperature of 45°F (7°C) when they will bloom late in January. *Scilla bifolia* has two bronzy-green leaves and bears 6–8 star-like flowers of gentian-blue on an 8-inch (20-centimetre) stem. There is a white form, *alba*, whilst *rosea* bears pale-pink flowers. *S. sibirica* blooms at the same time. It has 3 or 4 strap-like leaves and bears its drooping bell-shaped flowers on 8-inch (20-centimetre) stems. The best form is Spring Beauty which bears flowers twice the size of the type and of deep delphinium blue which last for weeks in a cool room. Use a 10-centimetre bulb for pot culture.

Tulip. For years, pots or bowls of dwarf single red tulips of Duc van Thol type have been grown in their thousands for the Christmas trade, the specially prepared bulbs being forced in a tem-

Early tulips in a cold frame. The boxes of tulips are filled up with soil

perature of 60°–65°F (16°–18°C), usually in boxes and transferred to bowls when just showing colour for this is one of the few bulbs that can be treated like this. Now, the high cost of providing such warmth has curtailed their growing yet the magnificent *greigii* and *fosteriana* tulips, which require virtually no artificial warmth to bring them into bloom, can be grown instead. True, they would not be in bloom for Christmas but should be by mid-February when they would be much appreciated. They are treated in the same way as other hardy bulbs and can be flowered in a cold frame; or they can be taken indoors, into a garden room or an attic with skylights and there brought into bloom with the minimum of heat, just enough to keep them comfortably grow-ing. Water sparingly, giving just enough to keep the compost moist.

The *T. greigii* hybrids have broad glaucous-green leaves heavily mottled with purple, brown or yellow which adds to the beauty of the plants. Red Riding Hood is one of the best for small pots (plant 4 bulbs into a 5½-inch pot) growing 8 inches (20 centimetres) high and bearing urn-shaped flowers of oriental red. Plaisir is of similar habit, the flame-coloured flowers shading to gold at the petal edges. Oratorio has flowers of strawberry-pink and those of Dreamboat are salmon-pink, shaded buff on the outside. Both are lovely under artificial light.

With but one or two exceptions, the *T. fosteriana* hybrids are taller-growing. Rockery Beauty, however, grows only 8 inches (20 centimetres) tall and has grey-green leaves above which it bears dazzling scarlet flowers with pointed petals. Cantaba grows 10 inches (25 centimetres) tall and also bears brilliant-red flowers and Golden Eagle, which grows to a similar height, is yellow with a scarlet "flush" or shading on the outside of the petals.

The bulbs cost between £5 and £7 per 100 wholesale and are obtainable in 25s at the 100 rate. Four planted in a short 5½-inch pot or bowl will cost about 25p and sold at 50p or 60p would show a useful profit.

After flowering, all these bulbs can be planted in the garden to bloom again the next year or they may be dried off in the pots and brought into bloom again the following year when they will do even better.

12

Ways With Dried Flowers

Where to dry flowers and leaves—Materials of field and hedgerow—Grasses for drying—Annual flowers to dry—Perennials for drying—Other methods of preserving—Pressing flowers and leaves

One of the most interesting and pleasant ways of making money at home is from dried flowers. It is a profitable hobby that can be carried out all the year round and there are many ways of making dried flowers help to pay the rent or rates. No special equipment is required but you will need a room to do the drying. This can be a dry cellar with a window or with alternative ventilation, or an attic or shed. An attic is perhaps the best place. Dried flowers, attractively arranged, can take the place of expensive out-of-season freshly cut flowers and they are just as attractive. Artistic arrangements of dried flowers will find a ready sale to banks and hotels for they retain their beauty for many months and are just as lovely as fresh flowers for they are indeed the flowers and grasses, fruits and foliage of hedgerow, field and garden and bear no resemblance to the artificial flowers so often used for decoration in hotels and restaurants. Fresh flower arrangements are not only expensive but need replacing at least once a week and this means time as well as money. Fresh flowers also need the daily topping up with water and the removal of those flowers which have died before their time and when labour is expensive, and often in short supply, public places are turning more to dried flowers. They would be more often used if available but the drying of flowers and foliage is now almost a lost art and yet like so many things long neglected, the art of working with dried flowers is returning to a society fast becoming cost-conscious.

But there is more to the art of working with dried flowers than hanging them up in an airy room for a few weeks. You will need to know which are the best materials to dry, those which retain their beauty the longest when dried and which flowers do not respond to their preservation by drying. There are those which improve when dried, taking on more intensive colouring than when fresh, whilst others drop their petals and become limp and uninteresting and have no use in dried flower arrangements.

Materials of Field and Hedgerow

Begin collecting flowers and foliage early in summer and continue to save and prepare them up to the beginning of winter. By early November you will have a large amount of material to use and during the winter months you will be able to make up artistic arrangements to sell or give as presents, also to use in your home when fresh flowers are expensive. They can be used in many ways besides making them into artistic arrangements; for making flower "pictures" of all sizes and shapes; for bookmarks and for decorating birthday cards and letter heads. Those who live in the country can search the hedgerows and fields for suitable material, beginning with violets in spring and ending with the fruits (berries) of wild roses, holly, hawthorn and even blackberries in autumn, which can be treated with glycerine or antifreeze and will retain their colour and form for many months.

Grasses and cereals, especially wheat and barley, are especially attractive after drying and there are many hedgerow plants which produce handsome seed heads which can also be saved. Poppies are especially attractive when the large green seed heads have formed, so too is Old Man's Beard, *Clematis vitalba*, which entwines about the hedgerows and in autumn produces shaggy white seed heads, appearing from a distance like the beard of an old man.

The field or red poppy takes its botanic name from the Greek *rhoia*, a pomegranate, for the large globular seed capsules are like miniature pomegranates.

The sea lavenders also lend themselves to drying as do all forms of statice. *S. limonium* has a leafless flower stalk at the top of which appears lilac-blue flowers in spreading clusters. It is in bloom July to October. It is closely related to Armeria, the thrift or sea-pink, a long-stemmed garden form which is useful for drying.

Several of the most useful flowers for dried arrangements are found close to the sea and in marshlands, amongst which are the rushes, the bulrush and greater reed mace, being especially handsome with their dark-brown flowers which are formed in cylindrical spikes at the end of 6–8-foot (2-metre) stems.

Some plants such as the Scottish thistle (Scotland's national emblem) and the great burdock are found on wasteland. Both are vigorous tall-growing plants well known to countrymen but not so well known to flower arrangers though they are most handsome when dry, the burdock with its bristly burrs which dry to a rich brown. With their hooked spines, the burrs attach themselves to one's clothes when thrown, a favourite country pastime of children through the ages.

Though in no way related to the burdock, the common dock whose leaves will relieve nettle stings when rubbed on to the skin, can be used by the flower arrangers for the whorls of seed heads turn deep crimson when the stems are dried in anti-freeze.

Another strikingly lovely seed head is that of the tree mallow which grows to 10 feet (3 metres) tall, its handsome rose-coloured flowers being replaced by silver seed heads.

These are some of the wild flowers, seed heads and fruits to be found in field and hedgerow and which are suitable for drying:

Plant	Common name	Part to use	When available
Arctium majus	Burdock	Burrs	Late summer
Clematis vitalba	Old Man's Beard	Seed heads	Autumn
Crataegus monogyna	Hawthorn	Fruits (berries)	Winter
Endymion non-scriptus	Bluebell	Fading flowers	Early summer
Lavatera arborea	Tree Mallow	Seed heads	Late summer
Onopordon acanthium	Scottish thistle	Seed heads	Late summer
Papaver rhoeas	Field poppy	Seed heads	Late summer
Rosa canina	Wild rose	Fruits	Late summer
Rosa rubiginosa	Sweetbriar	Fruits	Late summer
Rumex conglomeratus	Common dock	Seed heads	Late summer
Scirpus lacustris	Bulrush	Flower spikes	Late summer
Statice limonium	Sea lavender	Flowers	Mid-summer
Thypha latifolia	Great Reed Mace	Flower spikes	Late summer
Viburnum opulus	Guelder rose	Fruits	Late summer

Grasses for Drying

Many of the wild and cultivated grasses are most handsome when dried and used in arrangements and for making flower pictures. The various grasses and cereals used on their own are most attractive in vases. They may be grown in the garden where their beauty is also to be appreciated and, with some, the foliage is quite as handsome as the flower spikes. *Avena candida* has steel-blue foliage whilst Carex, Evergold, one of the sedges, has leaves margined with green and gold and bears its flowers in handsome panicles.

Many grasses of the countryside can be grown in the garden and there are others of ornamental value which come from afar, including the pampas grasses of Argentina and New Zealand. Most of the perennial grasses will form dense clumps after a year or two and can be propagated by division at any time between November and April. Many can also be grown from seed and this is how the annual grasses are grown, often from self-sown seed.

In the garden, sow in early spring where the grasses are to grow. If a border is available for growing all those plants to be used for drying, sow in circles of about 12 inches (30 centimetres) diameter, scattering the seed lightly over the surface and raking it in. Keep the soil moist and thin the plants if too thick.

Sow the taller grasses such as *Panicum violaceum* to the centre or back of the border and the most dwarf to the front, in the same way that one would plant a herbaceous border with perennial and annual plants. The grasses can be sown between annual plants and the perennial grasses can be used with other perennials. Again, the taller perennial grasses can be planted to the back or centre of the border if it is an island bed with the most dwarf to the front. One may have only a long, narrow border, perhaps at the foot of a sunny wall, in which to grow plants for drying and this will be a profitable way of using the ground. If a larger border can be planted, so much the better for then a wider variety of plants can be grown for drying. Unlike ferns, grasses need the sun to be successful.

Grasses should be cut when at their best, when in flower but before they begin to seed. The same can be said for all material to be used for drying. It is the same when putting fruits and vegetables in the freezer. They should always be at their best, not past it.

Annual Grasses:
   Agrostis nebulosa. This is one of the Bent grasses amongst which

are the perennial forms *A. palustris*, the March bent, and *A. canina*, the Brown bent, both of which bear their purple-green flowers in long slender panicles on 16–20-inch (40–45-centimetre) stems during July and August. The annual *A. nebulosa* grows to a similar height and is known as the Cloud grass, its delicately formed spikelets borne in spreading heads producing a cloud-like effect.

Briza maxima. One of a group known as the Quaking grasses for when in bloom the spikes are never still. *B. maxima* is the Great Quaking-grass, with 9–17 flowered spikelets which are held on footstalks so thin as to be almost invisible. It grows 16 inches (20 centimetres) tall and in August bears drooping spikelets of creamy-white.

Hordeum jubatum (Syn. *H. marinum*) The Squirrel-tail grass which bears an erect flower spike 2 inches (5 centimetres long), like a tassel or squirrel's tail. It is a member of the barley family and flowers in midsummer.

Lagurus ovatus. The Hare's tail grass, it is the only species of the genus, growing 12 inches (30 centimetres) tall with 1-inch (2.5-centimetre) long spikelets borne in crowded heads made up of thousands of soft white hairs. It grows in sandy places.

Panicum violaceum. It is one of the most beautiful of hardy grasses, growing 3–4 feet (1 metre) tall with pale-green lance-shaped leaves and in July it bears recurving plumes of green and violet. *P. crus-galli* is the Cockspur grass which grows to a similar height and bears its green spikelets in a branching pyramid.

Setaria italica. One of the Bristle-grasses and similar to Panicum. It grows 2 feet (60 centimetres) tall, its nodding pale-green flower heads later turning to golden yellow.

Tricholaena rosea. One of the most attractive of all grasses, bearing fluffy pinkish-brown spikelets at the end of 2-foot (60-centimetre) stems, hence its name of Wine grass.

Perennial Grasses for drying:
Alopecurus pratensis variegatis. The variegated Meadow Foxtail growing 20 inches (50 centimetres) tall. It forms a tuft of narrow leaves striped with yellow. The flowers are crowded into a spike-like panicle, like a fox's tail. *A. fulvus* is the orange foxtail, the creamily-white flowers turning orange as they age and are most effective in flower arrangements.

Arundo donax. The Provence reed of Southern France which in a moist soil will grow to 10 feet (3 metres) tall, bearing its glaucous arching leaves on long stems with the crimson flower spikes borne in a panicle 12 inches (30 centimetres) long.

Avena candida. It has steely-blue foliage which it retains all winter and in summer bears its spikelets in graceful arching sprays on 2-foot (60-centimetre) stems.

Cortaderia selloana (Syn. *Gynerium argenteum*) This is the Pampas grass of Argentina which in early autumn bears thick silvery plumes 12 inches (30 centimetres) long on stems 5–6 feet (about 2 metres) long. There is a pink flowered form, whilst Gold Band has broad golden bands on the leaves. The flowers are at their best in September when the stems should be cut. They can be dyed and are dried by standing the stems upright in large vases.

Helictotrichon sempervirens. Growing 3–4 feet (1 metre) tall, the large silvery panicles arise from tufts of glaucous leaves.

Kohleria glauca. It forms an evergreen tuft of glaucous green from which it sends up arching sprays of chocolate-brown plumes on 12-inch (30-centimetre) stems.

Lasiogrostis splendens. It forms a clump of graceful arching leaves from which arise stems 3–4 feet (1 metre) long at the end of which are large plumes (like those of Pampas grass) of a lovely shade of creamy-buff. Cut when at their best and dry as for pampas grass.

Miscanthus sinensis. A Japanese grass growing 6–7 feet (2 metres) tall, its broad arching leaves having a striking white vein down the centre whilst it bears plumes of dark velvet-red.

Panicum virgatum. A perennial growing 3–4 feet (1 metre) tall with gracefully recurving plumes of green and red.

Pennisetum rupellii. From a tuft of narrow bright-green leaves arise stems 3–4 feet (1 metre) long at the end of which are large purple plumes which arch attractively near the top of the stems. *P. orientale* is also valuable for cutting, its neat flowers being of bronzy-brown colouring.

Phalaris arundinacea. Known as Gardener's Garters, it grows 6–7 feet (2 metres) tall, its leaves being striped with yellow and its flowers are borne in long purple spikelets.

Stipa pennata. The Feather grass which bears graceful arching stems 2 feet (60 centimetres) tall which terminate in large feathery plumes.

The perennial grasses are propagated by division every 3–4

years when they will have formed large clumps. They can be divided into numerous crowns or offsets and replanted into soil which has been fortified with some old mushroom compost. Late autumn or spring is the best time to divide them and they like a soil containing some humus, one which is retentive of summer moisture. Grasses do not grow well in a thin, dry soil nor in shade.

The flower spikes should be removed with a pair of sharp scissors, cutting the stems as low down as possible. This will keep the plants tidy and there will be plenty of nice long stems for flower arrangements. The stems can be shortened as required.

As each grass reaches its best, cut the flowers as soon as the dew has dried off them. Do not cut them if wet with rain. Nor must they be allowed to run to seed. If growing grasses in the garden, it will not be difficult to keep each species to a separate bunch but this is not possible if cutting grasses from field and hedgerow. Tie each bundle of stems with raffia about 3 inches (7.5 centimetres) from the ends, making the bundles secure but not too tight and suspend them from a nail or from the rafters of an airy room or shed. It will take about a month to dry them off. They are then placed upright in vases and kept in a dry room away from sunlight which will bleach the attractive colourings.

Grasses can also be dried in trays on a bench, spreading them out thinly so that the air can reach each stem and flower head. Handle with care so as not to break off the heads. When dry, place upright in vases.

Annual Flowers to Dry

There are annual and perennial flowers suitable for drying and they can be planted in narrow borders with the grasses. Like the grasses, a number of them have handsome foliage which contributes to the garden display when the flowers are removed. Cut them when at their best, before they turn brown and begin to form seed heads, though some are more attractive when they had done just that.

Seed heads are gathered before they begin to shed their seeds and they must be inspected each day for their beauty will be lost as soon as they shed their seeds. The seed pods of lupins, if the stems are removed when the pods are filled with seeds but are still green, are attractive in arrangements and so are the seed capsules of field (red) and oriental or perennial poppies. The flowers are left on the plants to form seeds and are cut before the capsules turn brown when they will begin to shed their seeds.

One of the loveliest of all plants when its seed pods have formed is Honesty, a biennial which produces its seeds in a round moon-like capsule or case the size of a 10p piece. Inside two protective outer skins are two silver linings which are transparent and reveal the seed inside. Remove the stems when the pods are fully formed and hang up to dry like grasses. The brown outer skins will soon shrivel and can be carefully removed, leaving the two silver linings.

Acrolinium. It is almost hardy and is sown in spring where it is to bloom. Like all "everlasting" flowers it needs a sandy soil and a sunny situation. In warmer parts, seed can be sown early in September when the plants will bloom in July; those from a spring sowing in September. The plants grow 16 inches (40 centimetres) high and the variety *flore plena* bears double blooms of rose-pink. Cut when fully open with as long a stem as possible and dry in an airy room.

Helichrysum. Native of South Africa, the Straw flowers are amongst the best of the everlasting flowers for drying but are only half-hardy in the British Isles. They are sown in April where they are to flower. Sow thinly into ordinary soil but they need full sun to do themselves justice, otherwise much of the rich colour of the flowers will be lost.

For early bloom, sow the seed in March in gentle heat and transplant the seedlings when large enough to handle. Grow on until the end of April then move to a cold frame to harden off. Plant outdoors early in May, spacing them 8 inches (20 centimetres) apart.

The double-flowered strain of *H. monstrosum* is the best for cutting, the flowers having several rows of petals which crackle like dry papers when touched, and are obtainable in shades of yellow, orange, crimson and rose. The flowers are at their best early in autumn when they are cut just above soil level and taken indoors to complete their drying. As with all material for drying, do not cut them when damp with dew or rain. There are several perennial forms which are more useful in the garden on account of their silver foliage.

Molucella laevis. Known as Bells of Ireland this is an excellent plant for the flower arranger but the seed is difficult to germinate unless a temperature of 60°F (16°C) is provided by a propagating unit. Sow early in March and after hardening, plant out early in May 12 inches (30 centimetres) apart. It grows 3–4 feet (1 metre) tall, the stems being covered in green sheaths or flowers arranged all the way up and around the stem. Late in summer, cut the stems just above soil level and hang up in an airy room. In 3–4 weeks, the "flowers" (really bracts) become like paper and turn a dull yellow. They can also be preserved by immersing the stems in anti-freeze or glycerine for 2–3 weeks when the bracts turn bright yellow.

Rhodanthe. A half-hardy everlasting annual, with pretty pink flowers of paper-like texture which are cut late in summer and used in flower arrangements. *R. manglesii* grows 12 inches (30 centimetres) tall and can be sown where it is to bloom or it can be given half-hardy treatment, sowing in gentle heat and planting out in May after hardening.

Statice sinuata. It is a biennial form of statice but as it is only half-hardy in the British Isles is best treated as an annual, like helichrysum. It prefers a light, sandy soil and grows 18 inches (45 centimetres) tall. Plant out in May 12 inches (30 centimetres) apart and cut almost at soil level as soon as the flowers show colour. Fasten into bunches and hang up to dry. Best varieties are Market Rose and Blue, and Lavender Queen.

Xeranthemum. Native of South Africa, it is almost hardy and is usually sown in spring where it is to bloom. The daisy-like everlasting flowers are borne singly on 2-foot (60 centimetre) stems during August. They appear in shades of crimson, rose and pink and have an outer ring of petals and numerous petaloids at the centre. Thin the young plants to 6 inches (15 centimetres) apart and cut when the flowers have fully opened. String up in an airy room to dry.

Perennials for Drying

With but one or two exceptions, it is those perennials which bloom late in summer that are most satisfactory when dried. Most have attractive silver foliage which is a bonus when growing in the garden and when cut. They are dried by hanging up in an airy room and should be cut when the flowers are at the point of perfection and with as long a stem as possible.

Achillea eupatoria. A plant of extreme hardiness, it flourishes in ordinary soil and an open sunny situation and blooms August–October, bearing its flat heads of golden yellow on 3-foot (1-metre) stems. It is long-lasting in water and when dried. To dry, hang up the bunches in an airy room. The variety Coronation Gold bears flowers of deepest yellow whilst Moonshine is of more compact habit and bears lemon-yellow flowers. It has beautifully silvered foliage. Set the plants 2 feet (60 centimetres) apart between October and March.

Allium moly. It was grown in Elizabethan gardens and known as Golden Garlic. It is a bulbous plant and naturalizes well in a sandy soil and in a sunny situation when it spreads rapidly, soon covering a large area. It bears bright-yellow flower heads on 20-inch (45-centimetre) stems during June and July and they retain their colour when dried. It is one of the first flowers to dry in summer. *A. schoenoprasum*, the familiar chive, is not only useful when grown for its leaves which are cut into small pieces to include in soups and stews but the mauve flowers, like small golf balls and held on leafless 16-inch (40-centimetre) stems, can be dried.

Anaphalis yedoensis. The "Immortelles", so called because its small white flowers remain for weeks on the plants without their petals falling and dry perfectly when they are a pleasing foil for the richer-coloured flowers. It grows 2 feet (60 centimetres) tall with silvery leaves and bears its flowers in branched heads. The species *A. triplinervis*, Summer Snow, grows only 10 inches (25 centimetres) tall and also has silver foliage. Its papery white flowers which crackle when touched are borne in clusters. The plants require a well-drained soil and an open, sunny position.

Armeria formosa. The largest of the sea thrifts, bearing its ball-like flowers at the end of leafless stems 16 inches (40 centimetres) long and in shades of crimson, pink, salmon and mauve. It makes a large clump, comes into bloom in May and continues until late Summer. It can be cut and used fresh or after drying in an airy room when the flowers will retain their colour all winter. Plants are readily raised from seed sown in a frame or in boxes in the kitchen window, transplanting the seedlings to where they are to flower. Older plants are difficult to propagate.

Echinops ritro. The Globe thistles are handsome plants in the border with their silvery leaves and stems. *E. ritro* has leaves which are silvered only on the underside and in July and August bears purple spiky globes as large as golf balls on 3–4-foot (1-metre) stems. This is the time to cut them and suspend in an airy room to dry. *E. humilis*, Taplow Blue, grows to a similar height and has pale-blue flowers.

Eryngium. The Sea hollies are amongst the best of all plants for drying. They grow about 2 feet (60 centimetres) tall and propagation is by cuttings rooted in May or by seed sown at the same time. Like most plants used for drying, the eryngiums prefer a sandy soil and an open sunny situation. *E. oliverianum* has long spiny silvery leaves, like those of holly, and bears thistle-like flowers of deep blue on branched stems. *E. planum*, Violetta, has stems which are purple like the flowers.

Physalis franchetti. This is the Chinese Lantern or Cape Gooseberry for it is a native of South Africa and is edible. The dried flowers resemble paper lanterns and turn from yellow to blood red as they dry. The stems are cut close to the ground late in September when they are taken indoors to hang up for drying.

The plant grows from a creeping rootstock, like mint, and requires a moist, humus-laden soil and an open situation. They are best grown (like mint) in beds to themselves, planting the roots in spring, in trenches 4 inches (10 centimetres) deep. Spread the roots out well. If the plants receive plenty of moisture the stems will reach a height of 2 feet (60 centimetres) but only half the height if the soil is dry in summer.

Sedum. The stonecrops, so called because the most dwarf species grow in the mortar of old walls. They are succulents, able to store up moisture in their fleshy grey-green leaves on which they survive during times of drought. The border sedums grow best in a rich soil and require a sunny position. The best for drying is *S. spectabile*, Autumn Joy, which grows 2 feet (60 centimetres) tall and in autumn bears flat heads of salmon-red, turning to crimson with age and when they are cut.

Solidago. The Golden Rods are in bloom in late summer and autumn and if cut when nicely showing colour, retain their beauty when dried. They grow well in ordinary soil and in almost any situation and are propagated by root division. Lemore bears branching heads of primrose yellow on 30-inch (75-centimetre) stems and Cloth of Gold is golden yellow.

Stachys lanata. From its grey woolly leaves like pieces of felt, it is called Lamb's Ears. It is a handsome ground-cover plant in the garden whilst its poker-shaped spikes of purple and grey, borne late in summer, can be cut and dried for flower arrangements. It is a plant of easy culture and is readily propagated by offsets.

Statice latifolia. It grows 2 feet (60 centimetres) tall and requires a well-drained soil retentive of summer moisture when, from July until September, it will form billowing clouds of tiny purple-pink flowers and it dries perfectly. *S. incana* bears deep-pink flowers on 12-inch (30-centimetre) stems and needs a well-drained sandy soil and sunny position.

Flowers after drying should be stored with care for they will be brittle and must be handled carefully. They must be stored, if not in complete darkness, in subdued light for in sunlight they will fade. They can be kept upright, in tall vases or laid down on shelves. The large drawers of a cupboard or chest will be suitable for this will enable the flowers to be laid flat and will keep them free from dust. They should be kept in a dry but cool room for they will shrivel and disintegrate in a room with a too high temperature such as caused by central heating: 50°F (10°C) is ideal.

Other Methods of Preserving

There are certain flowers which can be preserved by other methods. These include rose buds, carnations and pinks, pansies and violas, zinnias with their petals of rubbery texture, sweet peas, and marigolds (calendulas). The flowers with their short stalks are covered with ordinary household borax. Place the flowers in shoe boxes, using a separate box for each flower, and arrange them in layers. Over each layer of flowers, sprinkle some borax over the petals, working it about the flowers (which must be cut when at their best) with a children's paint brush, for it is necessary that every part of each flower be treated. Turn the flowers over so that all parts are covered, then add another layer of flowers which must be quite dry when cut and are treated at once before they lose their freshness, and sprinkle more borax over them, gently working it about all parts of the flowers with the brush. Rose buds should be held with one hand and the borax sprinkled into them. Double carnations and pinks too are treated in the same way. It takes time and cannot be hurried. Use the borax generously (from household stores it is not expensive) and after treating the flowers, cover them with a 1-inch (2.5-centimetre) layer. Put on the box top to keep out the air then seal the boxes with gummed tape and move to a dry shelf or drawer. Again, do not place in too high a temperature. The flowers should be completely dry in 3 days and will have lost little or nothing of their colour and form. They will, however, be paper-like to the touch, having been completely dried off. After several days, remove the flowers and brush off the borax, placing the flowers in fresh boxes and keep them in a cool, dark place until required.

Leaves and berries and those plants which have bracts rather than flowers, such as Molucella, are best preserved by treating them with glycerine or motor car anti-freeze which is cheaper and more easily obtained than glycerine. The leaves of beech and berberis, blackberries and raspberries, rowan and oak, viburnum and silver birch can be treated and will turn a rich brown colour, some like milk chocolate, others cocoa brown, all of which are delightful when used with yellow flowers to create an autumn-like effect. Raspberry leaves turn crimson. Berries too, such as rose hips and the haws of the thorn, the berries of holly and firethorn (pyracantha), will retain their colour and form when given the same treatment which is to use 1 part of either glycerine or anti-freeze to 2 parts boiling water. Place in a bucket, mix well together and insert the stems of the leaves and berries to about 2 inches. The solution must be used when just off the boil other-wise it will not be absorbed by the hard-wooded stems. For smaller sprays use an earthenware jar. It will take 2–3 weeks for the solution to be absorbed, when the leaves will have turned a rich brown. Beech is the exception and will take only a week. At the end of the time, drops of moisture will appear on the leaves which will denote that no more solution can be absorbed by them. Remove them from the solution, dry off the moisture with a clean cloth and lay the stems on trays or shelves in a cool, dark place and use as required. If berries (on the stems) are sprayed with hair lacquer, this will prevent them losing their gloss.

Pressing Flowers and Leaves

Yet another way of preserving flowers and leaves is by pressing them. Flowers which open flat such as clematis and the poet's narcissus, single petals of tulips and roses and hydrangea florets, also pansies and violas and certain grasses, are the most suitable and those leaves which lie flat like those of ivy, clover, many of the scented-leaf geraniums and ferns of several species are the best for pressing.

Material to be pressed must be collected dry and should be placed between sheets of blotting paper, which is better than newspaper, but several sheets of clean tissue paper is almost as good. Have everything ready so that the flowers and leaves can be pressed almost as soon as gathered from garden or hedgerow. The simplest method is to place cardboard over the upper piece of blotting paper and on top of the cardboard to place heavy books or old weights which are kept in place for a month or more depending on the thickness of the flower and leaf to be pressed.

Flower presses made from two pieces of plywood (at top and bottom), with layers of cardboard between and held in place by a 4-inch (10-centimetre) screw with a regulating wing-nut at each of the four corners, are obtainable from stores which cater for children's requirements. At school, I made a tie press from two lengths of planed wood with cardboard and blotting paper between which worked on the same principle. It has since been in constant use for pressing flowers. Whatever method is used, the material for pressing must be carefully laid out so that none overlaps and all is enclosed by the press. If a press is used, place blotting paper between each layer of cardboard to absorb the moisture. When each layer is filled with material, put on the top piece of plywood and tighten the screws as evenly as possible all round so that the pressure is constant rather than concentrated at any one side. The layers should be made comfortably tight but not excessively so but the screws may need tightening slightly after about a week.

The longer that the material is left, the more satisfactory it will be. It should be left a month or more so that every scrap of moisture has been absorbed by the blotting paper. Then remove the material with care, using a fine stainless-steel knife blade and lay the material to be used for making birthday cards and pictures on sheets of clean white paper in a drawer. Keep pressed flowers dry and in the dark and in a temperature of about 50°F (10°C) just like any other dried material. Those who have nimble fingers and are artistic can turn the dried material to profitable use in many ways or they may know of a friend who could use the material better and share the profits, one doing the growing, harvesting and drying, the other the making up.

13

Ferns for Shady Places

Where ferns can be grown—Propagation of ferns from spores—Propagation by root division—Fern cases—Ferns in bottles—Hardy species and varieties for cases and pot culture

Most of the plants described in this book require either sunlight or artificial light in which to grow and for those who find difficulty in providing these, the culture of ferns will enable them to take up an interesting and profitable hobby. Ferns grow best in diffused light and there are many places to provide this requirement. At the side of a house in a built-up area may be a small piece of ground on which to erect a structure where ferns in pots can be grown and sold to garden shops and florists at remunerative prices. The ground may be on the side of the house which has a northerly aspect and where little else will grow; or there may be a courtyard to the property, surrounded by a high wall and where sunlight is virtually excluded. A fern house could be built as a lean-to along a wall facing north or east. Using 2-inch (5-centimetre) timber for the supports or uprights and 1½-inch (4-centimetre) for the frame, a simple fern house can be fixed to the wall and covered with heavy-duty white plastic material tacked to the frame on the inside and outside in place of glass. This would protect the less hardy ferns from frost damage in winter.

Hardy ferns may also be grown outdoors in narrow borders in a sunless courtyard or garden where little else will grow and the plants regularly divided and replanted in pots for sale, standing them on a sunless side of the house or yard which is not used for their open-ground culture. If there is room, a fern garden can be made against a wall by heaping up soil to a height of about 3–4 feet (1 metre) and inserting pieces of tufa stone into the soil at intervals. This will not only give the impression of ferns growing about shady outcrops as they do in the wild but the stone will retain moisture and keep the roots moist, a condition which most ferns require. The ferns too are most attractive when their emerald-green fronds are seen against the grey stones.

Wherever ferns are grown, the soil should contain plenty of humus so mix in some peat or leafmould or poplar bark fibre which is obtainable for the purpose. Peat brought from moorlands, containing the roots of heather and bracken, also old mushroom-bed compost or decayed manure, are suitable to dig in. There must also be a good depth of soil to prevent it from drying out too quickly in dry weather.

The raised ground of the fernery will permit those ferns requiring more moisture than others to be planted low down and those requiring less moisture to be planted at the top so that each will receive the conditions it most enjoys. To provide those plants with the damp conditions they need, ferneries of Victorian times were often built to a height of 20 feet or more and constructed with large pieces of stone which took two or three men to handle. From the top, water cascaded over the stones and with the spray, created ideal conditions for the ferns. It would cost some hundreds of pounds to create such a fern garden today but if the ground is well prepared and the plants are given a semi-shaded position, ferns can be grown just as easily on the flat.

Propagation of Ferns from Spores

Ferns are perennial plants with fibrous roots and with leaves (called fronds) simple or divided, curling inwards at the top. The stem which bears the leaf is called a stipe; the midrib a rachis; the leaflets are known as pinnae.

Ferns do not flower but reproduce themselves by means of seed-like bodies called spores (much like fungi) which can be observed on the underside of the leaves. Under suitable conditions, spores readily germinate, the small green body sending out tiny rootlets. The spores of mature fronds are shaken by tapping the fronds on to the level surface of a compost which is made up of sterilized soil and moist peat in equal parts. Compost to a depth of about 1 inch (2.5 centimetres) is placed over a similar depth of damp sphagnum moss obtainable from woodlands and which retains the necessary moisture for germination. After sowing, and do not cover the spores, immerse the bottom of the seed box in water and this is how it is always watered whenever the surface dries out. Covering the container with a piece of polythene will prevent too rapid evaporation of moisture.

The container can be placed in the kitchen window or in a greenhouse or frame and if the spores are sown in spring, they will germinate during the summer. In a propagating unit, however, germination will be rapid and even. As soon as the spores germinate and the small green bodies are seen, shade them from strong light and when large enough to handle, transplant to 3-inch (7.5-centimetre) pots. But it will take some little time for all the spores to germinate so do not be in a hurry to transplant them. It is usually better to let the containers remain untouched until the following spring which in any case is a better time to move the seedlings than autumn.

The potting compost is made up of equal parts of sterilized soil, sand and moist peat. Using a smooth-ended stick or cane, lift each tiny plantlet with care, taking with it, its tuft of fibrous roots and replant at once in the pots, taking care to cover all the roots and make it comfortably firm. Close the plants up in a frame or greenhouse and water with care, keeping the compost nicely moist but not wet and remember to shade them from strong light. During warm weather, admit plenty of ventilation and spray the plants often. If the transplanting is done in spring, by August the young plants will be ready to move to 5-inch (12.5-centimetre) pots. The compost should now be made up of 2 parts turf loam and 1 part each moorland peat, which will be black and contain the roots of dead bracken and heather, and sand. Mix well together before filling the pots. First crock them. Over the crocks place a 1-inch (2.5-centimetre) layer of damp moss. When removing from one pot to another, do not disturb the soil ball which will be full of roots. Remove it by tapping the pot and place it on a layer of fresh compost in the larger pot and pack the compost around it. For the winter, stand the plants in a greenhouse or frame or outside in a sheltered place. They will be ready to sell by next spring or summer.

Propagation by Root Division

An established plant can be propagated by division. Remove the plant from the pot and place it on a table or bench. The work can be done in the kitchen or cellar. Holding the plant firmly in the hands, tease apart the crowns dividing them in several pieces each with a bunch of roots. This is best done in spring. Each piece is replanted in a 5-inch (12.5-centimetre) pot containing the potting compost and grown on.

If placed in a shady position and kept moist, the plants will quickly make new growth and be ready to sell late in summer. Remember to pot the plants firmly, a most important factor when dealing with ferns and it is advisable to stand the pots on a bed of sand or ashes which will keep the pots clean and prevent weeds growing about them. During dry weather they will require plenty of moisture at the roots but from 1st October, any plants not sold will need very little water until the following spring. If placed in a greenhouse or frame, give them plenty of fresh air, except during severe weather, and water sparingly.

Rhizomatous ferns, those which produce a thick stem which creeps along the surface of the soil like Begonia rex, are also divided in spring. Each piece (of rhizome) that is pulled or cut away should have roots attached. These ferns require a more peaty compost, one made up of sterilized loam and moorland peat in equal parts and the rhizome is laid on the surface of the compost, covering only the roots and making the compost firm around them. Water in and stand outside in the shade.

Shirley Hibberd, a keen fern-grower of a century ago, advocated the need to study each fern in detail for all have different characteristics and need slightly different treatment. He gives as an example the dainty *Onoclea sensibilis* which increases by rhizomes from which arise new plants some distance from the parent. When in leaf, these are removed and potted separately.

Another method of reproduction is by bulbils which a few species such as *Crystoperis bulbifera* grow on the fronds. When large enough, they are detached and planted in seed pans in a compost made up of equal parts sterilized loam, peat and sand. Plant the bulbils 1 inch (2.5 centimetres) deep and 1 inch (2.5 centimetres) apart and keep them moist. The pan is best kept in a closed frame or in a shaded room when the bulbils will soon grow into little ferns and can then be moved to small pots and grown on.

Fern lovers should keep a look-out on bookstalls and in those shops dealing in old garden books for Shirley Hibberd's little volume *The Fern Garden* for although published more than a century ago it contains much information relevant to present-day gardening. His list of the twelve most satisfying hardy ferns to grow in pots formed the basis of my own collection some years ago and are worth listing here:

Asplenium viride	Green Fern
Athyrium filix-femina	Lady Fern
Blechnum spicans	Hard Fern
Cystopteris montana	Mountain Bladder
Lastraea dilatata	Broad Buckler Fern
Lastraea filix-mas	Male Fern
Polystichum aculeatum	Prickly Shield fern
Polystichum angulare	Hard Shield fern
Polystichum setiferum	Soft Shield fern
Scholopendrium vulgare	Common Hart's-tongue
Thelypteris dryopteris	Oak fern
Thelypteris phegopteris	Beech fern

For convenience, ferns may be divided into two main groups: (i) the rhizomatous ferns which require a dry situation and are found in the wild growing on old walls and about rocks high above the ground, and (ii) those which form crowns. These are frequenters of damp places and greater lovers of shade than those of group (i). Amongst hardy ferns of group (i) are these twelve:

Asplenium adiantum nigrum	Black Maidenhair
Asplenium ruta-muraria	Wall vue
Asplenium septentrionale	Forked spleen wort
Asplenium trichomones	Common Maidenhair
Ceterach officinarum	Scale or Rusty-back fern
Cryptogramma crispa	Mountain parsley
Cystopteris fragilis	Brittle bladder
Lastraea aemula	Hay-scented fern
Polypodium robertianum	Limestone polypody
Polypodium vulgare	Common polypody
Trichomanes radicans	Bristle fern
Woodsia ilvensis	Oblong woodsia

These ferns are also tolerant of chalk and limestone soils.

There are no ferns which like to be perpetually waterlogged. None grow in marshy ground but there are several which are often found by streams and in damp woodlands. Under cultivation, these six ferns require more moisture than others:

Athyrium filix-femina	Lady fern
Blechnum spicans	Hard fern
Lastraea thelypteris	Female buckler
Osmunda regalis	Royal fern
Onoclea sensibilis	Sensitive fern
Phyllitis scolopendrium	Hart's Tongue

Fern Cases

Those who wish to take up the specialized culture of ferns for pleasure and profit will find that there is a ready sale for ferns planted in glass cases, in addition to their sale as pot plants. The idea of growing ferns in cases was the invention of a Mr B. N. Ward, a surgeon of Finsbury Circus, London, who died in 1868, aged 88. His fern containers became known as "Wardian" cases and by the end of the century, at least one was to be found in almost every Victorian house. They became more popular even than the aspidistra and are now, more than a century after Mr Ward's death, becoming fashionable again for they do well in any room with diffused light.

A rectangular case as used for ornamental fish is ideal for ferns of compact habit. A sheet of glass can be placed over the top (leaving it slightly open at one end) to create a more humid

Ferns growing in a glass case as used for tropical fish

atmosphere and if placed in a shady room (where few other plants will grow) the ferns will require little attention apart from an occasional watering. They need to be divided and replanted only every 3 or 4 years. In Victorian times, fern cases were made to the most intricate designs and ideas, often at great expense and if one came up in an auction room today, it would command a great deal of money. But anything like the replicas of the Crystal Palace or the Brighton Pavilion in which to grow ferns and which at one time were the most sought after designs is quite unnecessary and would be tolerated in few homes today.

If you can make up a small rectangular fern case, ask your local florist who could take orders for delivery to the homes of his (or her) customers on a profit-sharing basis, to have it on display. Also, call and see your bank manager, building society secretary, and restaurant and public-house keeper with a view to making up a fernery to have on display in their premises. This could be supplied at no cost to them if they would pass on your name and address to those interested in buying one.

Fern cases can be made to all sizes from one say 15 inches by 10 inches by 10 inches high, which will give ample room for the growing ferns, to one 20 inches by 12 inches by 10 inches high. With the true Wardian case, it was possible to lift off the glass panels separately for each was enclosed in an iron or copper frame, the frames being held neatly together by hooks and eyes but this is not necessary and if a fish tank is used, the ferns can be tended from the top. Fern cases of Victorian times were often fitted with gas heating to enable the more exotic species to be grown whilst they were frequently moved from one house to another when it was usual for the well-to-do to move from towns to the sea in summer. The ferns could receive their owners' constant attention.

At the bottom of the case (or tank) place a 1-inch (2.5-centimetre) layer of washed shingle for drainage and over it add 2 inches (5 centimetres) of compost in which to plant the ferns. Use sterilized loam so as not to introduce pests or disease, some moist peat and sand in equal parts and mixed well together. Into the compost press two or three good-sized pieces of tufa stone so as to give a realistic appearance of ferns growing amongst rocks. Group the stones together near one end of the case and so arrange them that the top portion of the stones is as level as possible and grouped in descending or step-like fashion with the highest stone about 4 inches (10 centimetres) above the compost level. Tufa stone is the best to use for it is porous and the ferns love to get their roots into it. The stones retain moisture which is taken up by the roots.

Ferns from small pots but well established are used. They are set well into the compost with the soil ball level with the top of the compost. The artistic arrangement is all important. Plant several close to the stones, then plant others in small groups, those which are taller growing to the back of the case. Also, take into consideration the various leaf types. Some have attractively cut or divided fronds, others are more feathery whilst there are those with undivided tongue-like leaves. Those of neat, upright habit should be used in fern cases. Amongst the best are:

Adiantum venustum	8 inches	(20 centimetres)
Asplenium assimile	8 inches	(20 centimetres)
Asplenium attenuatum	10 inches	(25 centimetres)
Asplenium cristatum	10 inches	(25 centimetres)
Asplenium nitidum	6 inches	(15 centimetres)
Asplenium trichomones	4 inches	(10 centimetres)
Asplenium undulatum	9 inches	(23 centimetres)
Athyrium minutissimum	4 inches	(10 centimetres)
Blechnum penna marina	6 inches	(15 centimetres)
Doodia caudata	6 inches	(15 centimetres)
Lastraea acuminata	8 inches	(20 centimetres)
Lastraea glabella	8 inches	(20 centimetres)
Nimphobolus lingua	8 inches	(20 centimetres)
Nimphobolus pertusus	6 inches	(15 centimetres)
Pteris geraniifolia	9 inches	(23 centimetres)
Pteris leterophylla	6 inches	(15 centimetres)

These ferns can be obtained from specialist growers and many hardy ferns for growing in pots are obtainable from garden shops and nurseries such as Bressingham Gardens, Diss, Norfolk. Spring is the best time to make a start with their growing, when the plants are coming into new growth after their winter rest.

Ferns in Bottles

Ferns (and a number of other foliage plants of compact habit) lend themselves admirably to growing in glass containers such as sweet jars and bottles, even in a large wine glass which will make

Small bottle gardens: Asplenium fern is shown in a sweet jar and a wine glass

a pleasing table decoration for Christmas or other special occasions. Large green carboys made specially for the purpose or which have contained distilled water can be obtained for making a fern garden but they are expensive to purchase. They will, however, last a lifetime if carefully handled and can be placed on a table in the sitting-room or at one end of a counter in a bar or building society office where a bottle garden will cause much attraction. But any glass jar with a wide neck will prove satisfactory and will present little difficulty in its making. These fern cases in miniature will be a source of much interest if shown already made up to one's friends who will most likely place an order for one to be made for a birthday party table.

The opening at the top of the bottle should be not less than 2 inches (5 centimetres) wide but preferably wider, to enable pieces of tufa stone to be inserted in the bottle which will create a landscaping effect. But first thoroughly clean the bottle inside, then with a home-made stiff paper funnel, pour in a quantity of washed shingle to a depth of about 2 inches (5 centimetres). Then, using a long-handled wooden (or plastic) spoon, place in the bottle a piece of stone, its size and shape dictated by the size of the bottle neck. Perhaps it could be about 3 inches (7.5 centimetres) by 2 inches (5 centimetres), the narrow side going in through the neck and it can be manipulated into the right position when in the bottle. Keep it to one side or in a corner if the jar is square rather than in the centre and make it firm in the shingle. Afterwards, pour in the prepared compost to a depth of about 4 inches (10 centimetres). For ferns, use (where it can be obtained) moorland peat soil or mix together a compost made up of 1 part each sterilized soil, peat and sand. The compost should be in a friable condition: it should bind together when pressed in the hand but no moisture should exude. The compost can be firmed by nailing a piece of wood 1 inch (2.5 centimetres) square to the end of a long stick such as used for supporting indoor plants.

With the other end of the stick, make the first hole close to the stone to take the fern. This should have been grown in a small pot and have some of the compost removed if the bottle neck is quite small. Drop in the fern, roots downwards, and manipulate its roots into the opening in the compost by using the stick. Cover the roots with compost and using the other end of the stick, make it comfortably firm. Then put in another fern. The bottle may take 2 or 3 ferns: a carboy will take 4 or 5. Use only those of most compact habit and which grow upright rather than spreading. If two are being used, then let them be as diverse in their frond formation as possible and make the planting as artistic as space permits. If a large drinking glass such as a brandy glass is used, do everything in the same way but on a reduced scale and unless the glass is very large, use only one fern in each. The bottle or jar is best left open, otherwise condensation will form inside the container and collect on the sides, obscuring the view. The ferns will need just a few drops of water every 2 or 3 weeks but never over-water them. Keep the bottle away from strong light and if any fronds die back, remove them by inserting a penknife with a sharp blade, attaching the knife to the end of a stick and held firm by twine or wire.

Obtain any suitable jars you can find for the purpose (Heinz large salad cream jars are ideal) and with a little practice, you will be able to make up the most delightful miniature fern garden.

Hardy Species and Varieties for Cases and Pot Culture

Adiantum capillus-veneris. An evergreen, it is the true Maidenhair, present about damp rocks in south-west England and Ireland. It grows 8 inches (20 centimetres) tall, its fronds irregularly divided into alternate wedge-shaped leaflets. It requires warmth and ample moisture and does well in a case.

Adiantum venustum. Known as the Hardy Maidenhair, it grows 8 inches (20 centimetres) tall with delicate fronds of palest green and is seen to best advantage in a case.

Asplenium adiantum nigrum. The black-stemmed spleenwort which requires a soil containing plenty of peat for it likes acid conditions. Of tufted habit it grows 12 inches (30 centimetres) tall with glossy jet-black stems and twice- or thrice-pinnate fronds.

Asplenium cristatum. A form of Hart's Tongue fern which has unusual crests on the upper fronds. It grows 16 inches (40 centimetres) tall and requires a moist, shady place when in the open ground.

Asplenium ruta-muraria. The wall spleenwort which is found on rocks and old walls, growing 4 inches (10 centimetres) tall, its ovate fronds twice-pinnately divided into rounded lobes.

Asplenium scolopendrium. The Hart's Tongue fern which is one of the few ferns to grow well in a chalky soil. It grows 16 inches (40 centimetres) tall and does well in pots, bearing broad tongue-like fronds of sea-green and with parallel rows of spawn cases at right angles to the midrib. The form *undulatum* has waved fronds.

Asplenium trichomones. The Maidenhair spleenwort, it is of tufted habit and grows only 4 inches (10 centimetres) tall with a shining thin black midrib on each side of which are small deep-green lobes regularly arranged.

Asplenium viride. The green spleenwort which is distinguished from other spleenworts by its bright-green midribs. It makes a tufted plant 6 inches (15 centimetres) tall and does well in a case with its greater moisture.

Athyrium filix-femina. The Lady fern, found in damp wood-lands and bearing its lace-like emerald-green fronds at a height of 30 inches (75 centimetres). The form *minutissinum*, which grows only 4 inches (10 centimetres) tall, bears its tiny lacy fronds from numerous crowns. It goes not do well in a chalky soil.

Athyrium nipponicum pictum. The beautiful Japanese Painted fern which grows to a height of about 2 feet (60 centimetres), its silver-grey fronds having contrasting wine-red stems. It does well as a pot plant indoors.

Blechnum penna marina. A dainty fern for a case for it grows only 6 inches (15 centimetres) tall with deep-green fronds, beautifully cut like lace.

Blechnum spicans. The native Hard fern which has a rhizoma-tous rootstock from which arise erect fronds of brilliant green with brown midribs. It grows 16 inches (40 centimetres) tall.

Ceterach officinarum. The Scale or Rust-back fern, a familiar plant of old walls and which grows only 4 inches (10 centimetres) tall with pinnately divided fronds which have scaly stalks and, underneath the leaflets, rust-like scales are seen. A good pot fern it likes dry conditions.

Cryptogramma crispa. The Parsley fern which is present about rocky outcrops in northern England and Scotland, forming a dense tuft of brilliant-green divided fronds, like parsley. It grows 4 inches (10 centimetres) tall.

Cystopteris bulbifera. The Bladder fern of North America which forms low tufts of feathery green fronds. On the stems are numerous bulblets which are detached and grown on in peaty soil. It grows 8 inches (20 centimetres) tall.

Cystopteris montana. The Mountain Bladder fern of northern Scotland which grows 8 inches (20 centimetres) tall with triangular fronds four times pinnately divided.

Dryopteris filix-mas. The Male Buckler fern, its twice-pinnate fronds growing 2 feet (60 centimetres) tall and lance-shaped. It grows well anywhere and in any soil. The form *crispa cristata* grows to only half the height and has beautifully crested fronds which give it a light, feathery appearance.

Hypolepsis millefolium. The Thousand-leaf fern which grows 10 inches (25 centimetres) tall and has a creeping rootstock from which arise multi-leaf fronds which give it a lace-like appearance.

Onoclea sensibilis. The sensitive fern of North America, a dainty species growing about 16 inches (40 centimetres) tall with pale-green twice-pinnate fronds which are divided into lance-shaped leaflets (pinnae) waved at the margins.

Polypodium vulgare. The common polypody which is more tolerant of dry conditions than other ferns but a better pot plant is the form *pulcherrimum* which grows 10 inches (25 centimetres) tall and is evergreen whereas the Common polypody is not.

Polystichum aculeatum. The Prickly or Hard Shield fern, it requires acid peaty soil and is more tolerant of dry conditions than other ferns. The rigid lance-shaped fronds grow to 2 feet (60 centimetres) tall, the upper surface glossy pale green, the under surface covered in brown spiny scales.

Polystichum lonchitis is the Holly fern which grows 2 feet (60 centimetres) tall with long tapering pinnate fronds and is so called because the pinnae have sharp bristles along the edges.

Polystichum setiferum. The Soft Shield Buckler fern differing from *P. aculeatum* in having stalked, not sessile, pinnules whilst they are less stiff. It grows 3–4 feet (1 metre) tall. Less robust is the form *divisilobum*, one of the most attractive of all ferns for garden or pot culture for its pointed fronds are many times divided and present a light and feathery appearance. It grows to only half the height. The variety Herren Haussen is more compact still, its finely divided fronds being of bronzy-green.

Thelypteris dryopteris. The dainty Oak fern, distinguished from the polypodies in its smooth fronds which are divided into three branches each with 6 or more pairs of pinnules making it, in Shirley Hibberd's words, "extravagantly cheerful" in the home. It grows 6 inches (15 centimetres) tall.

Thelypteris phegopteris. The Beech fern, usually found in damp shady woodlands and like all Thelypteris, it is tolerant of a limestone soil. It produces its hairy fronds of delicate green to a height of 6 inches (15 centimetres). It makes a fine pot plant but it requires a moist atmosphere.

Thelypteris robertianum. The Limestone polypody, it is tolerant of most soils and grows well in sunlight and in shade. A short tufted plant with luxuriant foliage like that of the Oak fern but its fronds are covered in down which gives it a grey appearance.

Woodwardia radicans. Native of southern Europe it is hardy in the British Isles south of the Thames and makes an admirable pot plant. It sends up its graceful fronds to a height of 3–4 feet (1 metre). They are 12 inches (30 centimetres) broad with lance-shaped pinnae also 12 inches (30 centimetres) long. The variety *Cristata* has crested fronds.

Index